The Business, Banking
and Finance Collection
has been generously
donated by

Rick and Jan Ussery

TOO

STUPID

TO

QUIT

OTHER BOOKS BY RICHARD D. JACKSON

YESTERDAYS ARE FOREVER
A RITE OF PASSAGE THROUGH THE MARINE
CORPS AND VIETNAM WAR

THE LAST FAST WHITE BOY
A MEMOIR OF ATHLETICS IN THE FIFITIES
AT MARSHALL COLLEGE

TOO STUPID TO QUIT

BANKING AND BUSINESS LESSONS LEARNED THE HARD WAY

BY

RICHARD D. JACKSON

authorHOUSE™

1663 LIBERTY DRIVE, SUITE 200
BLOOMINGTON, INDIANA 47403
(800) 839-8640
WWW.AUTHORHOUSE.COM

First published by AuthorHouse 01/19/05

ISBN: 1-4184-5706-X (e)
ISBN: 1-4184-2927-9 (sc)
ISBN: 1-4184-2926-0 (dj)

Library of Congress Control Number: 2004092218

Printed in the United States of America
Bloomington, Indiana

This book is printed on acid-free paper.

First Edition

Cover art: THE LEADER, used with permission of Rosie Clark an Atlanta Artist.

The John Deaver Drinko Academy
For American Political Institution and Civic Culture,
Marshall University
Huntington, West Virginia

Author contact: dickjackson@mindspring.com

FOR

THOSE WHO HAVE
THE "GUTS" NOT TO QUIT.

AND

MARSHALL UNIVERSITY
FOR SUPPORT AND ASSISTANCE.

"A good banker should be bald,
overweight, and have hemorrhoids.
Baldness conveys maturity.
A paunch reflects wealth.
And hemorrhoids give a look of
concern to one's eyes."

Advice given to a bank trainee

AuthorUnknown

Contents

**Author standing in front of bombed-out stadium
Hue, South Vietnam in 1967.**

Author's Note

I served eight years in the United States Marine Corps, from 1960 to 1968, achieving the rank of Major.

From that time forward until 1995, I worked with six different companies in Georgia, ultimately serving as the chief executive officer of a commercial bank, First Georgia, a Federal savings bank, Georgia Federal, and finally as a vice-chairman and the chief operations officer of an information services company, First Financial Management Corporation, Inc.

My 27-year business career was spent in Atlanta and concluded in 1995, when I retired two months prior to the sale of my last employer.

With the exception of the United States Marine Corps, none of these organizations exists in name today. They were all acquired by larger organizations.

First Georgia and Georgia Federal Banks are now part of the Wachovia Corporation. Both of these companies were initially acquired earlier by The First Union Corporation. First Union and Wachovia subsequently merged and retained the name of Wachovia. First Financial was ultimately purchased by First Data Corporation.

A quarter of a century of my life was devoted to the banking industry. Those organizations under my control were considered to be very competitive, unusually creative, and highly aggressive with the banking methodology and management approaches employed.

The tactics employed in this traditional and conservative industry were abnormal or "outside the box" for many bankers.

As a result, a few business writers called me the most "Unlikely Banker" they had ever seen. Their observation did not surprise or disappoint me.

Background

The noted and famous economist John Kenneth Galbraith humorously stated: **"Banking is a career from which no man really recovers."**

Mark Twain offered his insight on the industry when he said: **"A banker is a fellow who lends you his umbrella when the sun is shining and wants it back the minute it begins to rain."**

I won't attempt to validate the accuracy of either statement here. However, after spending over 25 years in this occupation, whenever asked to denote my greatest accomplishment my standard response has always been **"I was never indicted."**

Unfortunately, several of my cohorts in the industry did not fare as well during the turbulent eighties and early nineties before the regulators began to ask questions, which should have been raised earlier about asset quality and accounting procedures.

Nevertheless, my response seems to satisfy most inquiring minds and after a slight pause the conversation always turns quickly to more mundane subject matter. This is more than suitable to me, since I don't relish entering into a topic that few people understand, and most find either uninviting or uninteresting.

However, the banking industry does offer a myriad of interesting and challenging opportunities for those pursuing a career in the financial services arena. Notwithstanding, of course, the challenge of maintaining a positive upward trend of growth and profitability in the uncertain, paradoxical, and quixotic economic times that consistently plague the industry over various "boom and bust" business cycles.

An example of these influences is the economic law of supply and demand. There are some pundits today who will tell us this age old-law has been repealed, because of the expanding worldwide economic climate and the dynamic rate of change now occurring in the business world.

Other factors unquestionably bear great weight on the industry, including recessions, depressions, and the push-pull effects of inflation, deflation, and political policies of some administrations, such as those supposedly based on "voodoo economics," a political term originating in the Ronald Regan era, by the opposition, to identify his economic policies.

Governmental budgetary practices, such as spending, taxing, and pork barrel projects to influence various contingencies weigh on the financial capability and stability of the banking world.

Regulatory policies and actions initiated by the powerful Federal Reserve System also affect bankers in their role to maintain orderly and positive growth cycles throughout the maze of these actions or inaction, whichever may be the case.

All of these factors influence the banking environment, like storms across the sea, creating high tides of anxiety and subsequent troughs of economic tranquility.

Bankers, or financial gurus, if there are such people, must steer through these waters with their craft floating upright and secure. They never know when the next giant wave might suddenly appear and capsize their small dinghy or luxury liner of financial services, sending it to the dark bottom to join other sunken or defunct organizations.

If bankers manage to avoid all these perils and finish their careers with their honor and credibility intact, they did a damned good job and should be proud of their accomplishments. If they subsequently went on to other ventures or responsibilities they probably did well, thanks to their training and acquired crisis management temperament, which is a way of life in this industry.

In essence, most bankers probably do recover from their banking careers, in contradiction to Professor Galibraith's earlier statement. I did after performing in the role of the CEO of a commercial bank for twelve years and a Federal savings bank for seven. However, my wife did seem to think a few quirks developed in my personality and temperament, which she was convinced resulted from my tenure in the banking industry.

But I attempt to blame any of my obvious deficiencies on the Vietnam War, my former job environment, prior to becoming a banker. I will also inform most people, whenever asked about any business success, such as it was, resulted from the training and experiences encountered during my eight years in Uncle Sam's fighting elite, The United States Marine Corps.

My rationale for this explanation is quite simple. Survival training, a disciplined lifestyle, leadership responsibilities as a troop leader, combat experience in the jungles of Vietnam, and other demanding military requirements heavily influenced my personal demeanor, mental toughness, and ability to adjust to a changing and complex business environment.

I must admit it was terribly difficult at times to translate these skills into readily acceptable business practices. Also, I found it challenging while making adjustments in my behavior to fit the corporate mold of some organizations. Nonetheless, these characteristics were ultimately accepted by my contemporaries and those who stood above me with great corporate visage and supreme authority.

Upon my initial entry into the banking scene in 1968, after returning from Vietnam, there were nearly 15,000 commercial banks and 5,000 savings and loans, S&L's or thrift institutions, as they are also called, in the United States.

Over the next several years the number of banks declined by one third, due to mergers and bank failures. For the same reasons, the numbers of savings and loans declined by approximately 60%, to 2,000 institutions. However, the failure rate in this industry component was much higher than the banking sector, because of certain regulatory limitations, mismanagement, greed, and illegal practices.

New regulations, promoted by various governmental agencies, began to flow into the financial services industry in the early eighties to broaden the business opportunities for financial institutions and make them more competitive.

Unfortunately, some managers did not know how to use these powers of expansion for their product lines and business plans effectively, or how to position their companies to compete on a more level playing field with their competitors.

At that time, barriers of entry for both old and new product offerings were eliminated, such as the restriction of paying fixed, or regulatory-mandated interest rates on various maturities of deposit accounts.

When the new money market account was introduced in the early eighties, after the regulations had been changed, some institutions initially offered these accounts in their markets with a high double-digit introductory rate. Rates had normally been paid in the 4 to 8% ranges for similar depository accounts.

Deregulation or re-regulation of the financial industry as it was sometimes called, provided many opportunities for those who could manage and control their organizations in this new era.

Prior to these regulatory changes, only a quarter-point differential in interest rates was allowed on most depository accounts between the bank and thrift industries.

The higher rate could be paid on deposits by the thrift banks to help them generate deposits for loans, because they were primarily home mortgage lenders and the preservation of this business segment was critical to our Nation's welfare.

In the sixties and earlier, most S&L loans were of a fixed- rate nature, and this rate differential on deposits was designed to give them an advantage in raising funds to support their lending efforts for this important market segment.

No interest was paid at this time on demand deposits (checking accounts), which helped financial institutions maintain a lower cost of deposits for lending purposes. This obviously enhanced the profitability equation for the financial services industry. However, this benefit would eventually dissipate in the eighties with the introduction of money market accounts and demand by customers to earn a fair return on all the deposits held by the bank on their behalf.

Times were changing rapidly in the world of banking and finance. It would be fair to say that many of the "old time" banking executives were not quite certain as to the methods they should use to restructure their organizations, business strategies, and product lines in order to prosper and survive in this dynamic and evolving environment.

The banking industry was in the process of being reinvented upon my accidental entry in the business.

Actually, I never considered the possibility of employment as a banker, because my youthful perception of most bankers was tainted. In my view they appeared to be unexciting, staid, and primarily "blue bloods" from wealthy families.

There was probably no real basis of fact for this conclusion. But the bankers I met seemed to epitomize these characteristics in my hometown of Huntington, West Virginia, where I attended school through the twelfth grade, and in 1959 graduated from Marshall College, now Marshall University.

This perception of the industry remained with me until actually making the choice to become a commercial banker, after completing eight years of duty in the Marine Corps in 1968.

It ultimately became evident that banking offered many varied and interesting opportunities for those willing to work hard and apply themselves to the challenges of this business. I gravitated easily and enthusiastically to those challenges that were newly exposed to me.

This attitude would remain the same over the next 26 years, while pursuing my passion and desire for a successful business career.

Fortunately, I could not have made a better decision, although the road was bumpy and frustrating. Some of my earlier perceptions would haunt me when encountering and trying to change some old traditions. Particularly, the "we-have-always-done-it-this-way" attitude. However, this aspect is prevalent in many industries and companies. The reality and abundance of internal politics and turf protection that was embedded in some institutions was also an eye-opener.

But these old practices were quickly changing, as the requirement for dedicated and hard-working professionals took on more importance, replacing nepotism and the status quo in order to meet the needs of this highly competitive and evolving industry.

I made my way through this forest of change, adapting and learning as much as possible. With luck, fortitude, inspired employees, and talented executives, my banking career was concluded in 1993 after serving seven years as the chief executive officer of Georgia Federal Bank, which was based Atlanta.

Prior to that assignment, my position for 12 years was as the chief executive and president of First Georgia Bank, a commercial bank, also in Atlanta.

My initial entry into banking occurred upon joining The First National Bank of Atlanta as an officer trainee at age 31, fresh from the Marines, and probably one of the oldest "trainees" to ever enter banking. Most of my contemporaries were at least five years younger. This disparity in age, background, experience, responsibility, and general demeanor created some gaps and obstacles for me in those initial years.

Unfortunately, my age and background placed me somewhat out-of-step with my business associates and contemporaries. Everyone seemed to either be a little younger or a little older in the different social and business circles of my membership. In addition, they were also much more business savvy.

My years of banking in Atlanta were full of challenge and replete with the requirement for continuing education. The leveling of the playing field, which was a regulatory thrust to help banks become more competitive with other financial intermediaries, produced a swirling environment of constant change and adjustment.

Admittedly, I have addressed this subject through my own experiences and reflections as I saw and lived them during my business career. Obviously, there is always room for error, misinterpretation, and accuracy of perception in any story.

My apologies are presented for any incongruities presented here. But, let me remind the reader that a person's perception is his own reality. Consequently, this story primarily reflects my view and understanding, while experiencing and responding to the opportunities and challenges.

Whether we are writing a check for payment, using a credit card for a purchase, protecting our valuables by using a safe deposit box, financing an automobile or borrowing millions of dollars to finance a business venture, we employ the services of a financial institution.

Without realizing it, we can be seriously affected in our personal or business transactions by the machinations of the institution, the gyrations of the economy, the market forces of the competition, and the monetary policy and regulations promulgated by the Federal Reserve System.

We are inextricably intertwined with the financial services industry, and the more we know about its operations, products, and motivations should be helpful when considering our future banking and financial endeavors.

This book will help explain how many of these forces interact, and provide insight and discussion on some very unusual management practices.

Perhaps, the next time you visit your favorite bank you will examine it a little differently. Possibly, you might want to ask questions about the institution to ensure that you can maintain some control over your financial destiny.

You may want to know something about the management, general-banking practices, and how the bank fulfills its fiduciary responsibilities to the stockholders and customers.

You just might develop a new perception about the organization, the services provided, and the people who conduct business for the company.

If management and organization principles interest you, there is an abundance of creative ideas and practices presented in this book. These should be helpful to both the novice and experienced practitioner.

Enjoy the trip. You will find this to be a very different view of the world of banking.

Chapter One
Destiny

Destiny has a way of interceding in a person's life in the most unusual manner, and at times when least expected. Some people say we establish our own life's direction, others contend things happen for various reasons outside of any person's control. Some believe all events are predestined and there is little we can do to influence the outcome of our lives or our futures.

When looking back and reexamining my life and the choices made or not made for that matter, there is an obvious connection between those decisions and the ultimate affect they had on my destiny.

Unfortunately, I didn't come to fully appreciate how much we predispose our futures by the actions we take, even very early in our lives, until recently. Cause and effect is a common analytical approach, but applying it to my life doesn't seem appropriate for me, when evaluating the course subsequently chosen and traveled throughout my career.

Most people must live through their mistakes, errors of judgement and successes to fully understand how the decisions they make and the subsequent action shapes the outcome of their personal situation.

To illustrate: I recall a television program years ago, which featured the comedy of Amos and Andy, two black comedians, who were always getting into some kind of mischief, regardless of their good intentions.

Andy was always in trouble and on one such occasion he went to Amos to seek his advice about a problem he had created for himself.

Amos provided a recommendation that Andy followed and he escaped from the troublesome situation. Later, Andy asked Amos how he had acquired such **"good judgment."** Amos thought about it for a while and then responded, **"experience."** Andy then questioned him as to how he had acquired so much experience. Amos's quick retort was **"bad judgment."**

I came to the realization, after many questionable choices on my part, that a person learns more from the mistakes they make, the games they lose, and the failures they experience, than from succeeding or winning on a regular basis. Losing causes many people to make an extra effort, mentally or physically, to overcome the deficiency in their judgement or performance at the earliest or next best opportunity

Winning and success does not necessarily cause people to mentally evaluate their performance or decision making, but is more likely to result in the pure enjoyment of the moment and mental satisfaction of their accomplishment, without evaluation of the reasons of why or how it happened.

Think about it. How did you learn? When did you learn? What were the driving forces that caused you to redouble or triple your efforts in the pursuit of your goals? Those decisions you made long ago; did they come back to haunt you or did they help you in your life's quest?

Our fears, judgements, needs, and motivations are all important in establishing the course we ultimately travel in pursuit of our dreams and passions. Our accomplishments, large or small, are the results from those actions. Did you ever attempt to rationalize your decisions and the effect they had on you? Did you make changes when things didn't go the way you wanted or did you just "ride the tide" and hope for the best? The answer to those questions most probably influenced your destiny.

Hindsight is always 20-20. Most of us are experts at being Monday-morning quarterbacks, and we can always call the right plays after the game has been played. We cannot allow ourselves to be stymied by inaction, as we play in the game of life, and avoid making decisions on a timely basis, because of the fear of failure, misdirection or criticism.

We can go to bat everyday, if we choose, and take our swing at the best opportunity. If we don't hit the ball or it doesn't go in the right direction, we can go up to bat again and take another cut at the next pitch.

If you keep swinging, eventually you are probably going to get some hits. True, you will also strike out a bunch of times, but you only hit the ball when you take the bat off your shoulder and swing at the pitch.

There is an old adage that runs: "Behold the turtle; he only makes progress when he sticks his head out of his shell."

Without question, I must admit taking more than my share of opportunities at bat and have struck out more times than the average person. Also, my head has been exposed or stuck out many times, which resulted in the receipt of some strong blows to both my ego and reputation.

Other times, progress was made, even in the face of adversity. On occasion, my efforts were not so good. These failures or personal setbacks were, in my mind, character-building opportunities.

Some of my close friends seem to think my past actions has produced enough character for me to last a lifetime.

You are probably asking, "What's your point and where are you going with all this destiny stuff?"

It has taken me many years to understand how my actions and decisions influenced my life, both as a young man and later as an older, and hopefully, more mature person. It should be helpful for me to explain my perception on this matter. Additionally, it is important to build a framework of understanding regarding those things we do and how our actions or failure to act impact our destiny.

For example, my entry into the banking world was quite accidental and will serve as a perfect illustration of my point. After leaving the Marine Corps in 1968 and participating in several interviews with prominent companies, I accepted a position with Boise Cascade in West Memphis, Arkansas, and began training in a fiberboard manufacturing plant working on a machine that produced cardboard paper for making boxes.

The assignment looked interesting and manufacturing appealed to me, because it appeared to offer excitement and lots of action. My vision and hopes were to use the skills learned in the Corps and eventually become a "Captain of Industry," just as I had been a "Captain of Marines."

Unfortunately, it didn't take much time to realize a horrible mistake had been made in my choice of jobs, even after giving it a great deal of thought and conducting research on the various available job opportunities. I discovered that I had misjudged my qualifications, capabilities, and most importantly those things that stimulated me mentally.

I found myself bored with the work, the environment, my fellow blue-collar employees, and had a difficult time comprehending the machinery and workflow. It just wasn't my thing. After just a few weeks it was apparent a conversation was needed with the assistant plant manager about my quandary.

He was an elderly gentleman and a very understanding and perceptive person. Interestingly, after explaining my issues, he told me to consider seeking employment with a bank. A position with a small financial institution, he commented, would allow more involvement and a broader insight with the different aspects of the business world. He also told me it would allow me to use my acquired people skills with both the employees and customers.

3

There were only two courses of action available. Continue with my present job and hope to find satisfaction and subsequently become a plant manager, which was my original goal envisioned upon accepting the position. My other choice was to seek different employment, before becoming totally dissatisfied and frustrated with the job and myself.

This feeling of failure in my initial job was disheartening. The wrong decision in pursuing my new career had obviously been made. I began to question my motives for leaving the Marines, especially since my recent selection for promotion to a Major. This new rank would have provided a nice pay raise with more career opportunity and increased job security.

The thought of moving my family again, even though we were not settled in a house, was repulsive. They had been through a great deal of stress during the previous two years. Starting with the notification of orders directing me to Vietnam, followed by their relocation from Oahu, Hawaii to Charlotte, North Carolina, and now after fourteen months of anxiety about my safety in the war, another move to Memphis, Tennessee.

Upon receiving orders to Southeast Asia, my wife, and former college sweetheart, Libby, decided to relocate our family to Charlotte, because it was a convenient point between our parents' homes.

We purchased a small house for them to live in during my absence. It was essential for me to make certain that if anything happened to me in Vietnam they would be in a stable environment, with caring people around, to help mitigate trauma and facilitate any necessary transition.

The house cost $13,000 and we obtained a 6% mortgage with a $500 down payment. Our monthly installment payment was only $106. This was certainly a sign of those times financially.

That was all we could afford on my salary and meager savings from seven years on active duty. A year later, after returning from Vietnam, we sold it for about the same price. It wasn't much of an investment, but it served the purpose and provided a nice home for my family during my absence overseas.

With that done, after several weeks traveling and visiting relatives, house hunting and moving, I caught a military aircraft out of Charlotte and flew to Camp Pendelton, California for a month of indoctrination training before deployment to South Vietnam.

Upon returning home fourteen months later, after the completion of my tour of duty, an active job search was initiated. If my memory serves me correctly, I spent no more than three weeks living in our family's home during the entire time we owned the house.

With my discontent growing daily on the job, the classified section on employment in the Memphis newspaper became my daily friend. After a couple of weeks scrutinizing the paper, an advertisement for management engineers caught my eye.

Immediately responding to the telephone number listed in the paper, diligently seeking an interview and providing information on my previous employment history, the individual listened carefully. Finally, after all my rambling he said, "Your background sounds interesting. Why don't you come by and see me?" We arranged a time to meet at his motel in downtown Memphis the next day.

He was a senior executive from The First National Bank of Atlanta, who was conducting interviews for the purpose of locating candidates to fill several different positions within his operations division.

His name was Duane Hoover. He was a graduate of Georgia Tech, and was one of the top officials of the bank. But, more importantly for me, he had spent some months in the Marine Corps and this connection opened the door for my interview.

The old, but often used slogan of the Marine Corps, "Once a Marine always a Marine," never seems to fail in any type of relationship between former members of this organization.

Because of his previous military experience he understood the significance of my background, training, personnel experience as a troop leader, and the responsibilities that most officers of in my rank were required to handle.

The interview was promising and my enthusiasm was certainly at its zenith. It had to be, because there was no business acumen on my part for him to evaluate. At the conclusion of our discussion he offered me the opportunity to travel to Atlanta for a bank visit and further personal evaluations.

Two weeks later the remaining interviews were concluded with the designated bank executives and they presented me with an offer to join the bank, as a management trainee, in Mr. Hoover's operations division.

During the interviews in Atlanta it was abundantly apparent the bank was progressive and was one of the largest in Atlanta. The business environment was highly professional, with a broad variety of employment possibilities, and the opportunity for on the job training was emphasized. This aspect was most appealing to me, because of my lack of business experience.

5

My wife, with my concurrence, decided it was the correct thing to do. We liked the idea of living in such a vibrant and growing city. I tendered my resignation to the Boise Cascade plant manager, who probably thought it was a good decision, and we were on our way to a new, and hopefully, a more fulfilling life.

There were important lessons in this decision-making process, which would have a major impact on my future destiny.

It was possible for me to have remained in my current position and perhaps eventually been happy and successful. Time would have answered that question. However, the way things were headed in my job, coupled with my overall dissatisfaction, it did not appear that the road to future success with my current employer was likely.

"Discretion being the better part of valor," I chose not to battle the demons and made a change, rather than stay on the job and hope for the best.

It is impossible now to know what the final outcome might have been with Boise Cascade. However, at that time I was one "unhappy camper," with a dismal view of my future in the business world.

It was critical for me to take charge, regardless of the pain and discomfort, and get on with my life. It was important to control my destiny now, or later suffer the indignities of failure at some point in my career. Fortunately, the decision was made without realizing the consequences at the time, and the result ultimately opened a New World for me to explore.

Never accept the apparently inevitable; if it is not what you want, do something about it. You can, if you are willing to take some risks and do your homework. You are limited only by what you think you cannot do.

You never know when or where the next opportunity might surface. Mine came from the newspaper, an unlikely source for the position I was seeking.

Keep your options open and try as many different approaches as you can conjure up in your mind. One point is certain and absolute; if you don't try you will not be successful. If you want a different outcome from the present, take action and direct your destiny.

Durwood Fincher, "Mr. Doubletalk," a noted and well-respected corporate humorous speaker from Atlanta, made a great point on this issue in a motivational speech to my bank employees at one of our meetings. He said; **"If you always do what you always did, you'll always get what you always got."**

My banking career started in March 1968 at The First National Bank of Atlanta as a 31-year-old trainee.

Although pleased to have this opportunity to learn business in a sophisticated financial environment, and delighted with my decision in general, I missed the camaraderie of my friends in the Corps, the exciting adventures, and the extensive responsibilities that had been part of that life.

Nonetheless, my new assignments were undertaken with renewed enthusiasm. First, selling a newly introduced credit card for several months to local merchants, and later heading a team to install a new computer system.

It was a very basic IBM model 20-card system, which replaced outdated tabulating machines that were used by the trust department for billing and customer reporting purposes.

Never in my past experiences had a computer been a part of my education prior to joining the bank. I possessed no concept of the operation and was amazed and confused with this technology. Although this particular system was very basic, its concept was almost incomprehensible to me.

Some years later I recall reading that there were no more than a few dozen computers installed in corporate America in the late fifties during my college years. Unfortunately, there was no opportunity presented to me to learn about them or see one in operation while in college or the Corps.

This initial assignment would be a revelation for me. Interestingly, my entire career in the financial services arena would ultimately evolve around this revolutionary and rapidly expanding business tool.

After these assignments, the responsibilities for managing several different departments in the data processing division were handed to me. My learning curve was vertical. The education and the stress created by the dynamics of this work environment was exciting and challenging.

Naturally, it was quite different from my previous experiences, but it was still mentally stimulating and personally motivating. Fortunately, I had either been born with or acquired early in my life an adrenaline need for change and excitement to keep me focused. Some people possess this drive. Many do not. Sometimes it's a good thing and other times it can be a liability. Depends on the person and how they mentally react to the stimulus.

Destiny has a funny way of influencing a person's life. My background, previous training, education, and the Marine Corps were not the typical building blocks in the preparation process, mindset, and creation of a management style for a future banker.

Nonetheless, they served me well in the business world and acted as enablers for a different kind of management approach with my future banking organizations.

Those companies were considered to be colorful, unorthodox, and creatively different from the normal conservative and often bland institutions in the market.

We learned to live by our "wits," and to conduct many of our business activities **"Outside the Box"** in order to grow and survive in the competitive Atlanta market.

As a result of this propensity of doing the unusual in my banking positions, people often frequently referred to me as an **Unlikely Banker,** who somehow had accidentally entered a conservative industry filled with an abundance of restrictions and regulatory oversight.

Obviously, these eccentricities and anomalies in the banking world didn't seem to make sense in such a traditional and structured environment to most people, especially my fellow bankers.

Chapter Two
An Unlikely Banker

My first experience with a bank occurred upon visiting my Aunt Lola, who worked in the administration offices at the First National Bank of Huntington, in my early years at St. Joseph's grade school. At that time, 1947, it was the largest bank in West Virginia and Huntington was the largest city with a population of 90,000 people.

The bank was located on the corner of Tenth Street and Fourth Avenue in the center of the business and shopping district. It was the tallest building in Huntington with typical high ceilings in the main banking area and glossy granite floors. Steel bars surrounded the teller windows to protect them from prospective bank robbers. Openness and ease of customer access, within the main banking room, was not promoted in those days of yore.

I can also recall seeing these very important, serious-looking men, who seemed large in stature, somewhat pasty in skin tone, and impeccably dressed in dark suits and white shirts. They were wandering around the area greeting various customers, probably their large depositors, while sternly observing every move of the staff, while they meticulously performed their duties.

Much of the time I tried to avoid these officials, lest their wrath would fall on my small persona and they would have me hauled away by the armed guards, who patrolled the banking floor looking for suspicious people like me.

In their eyes, my countenance probably resembled some small near do well, who was "eyeing the place," while planning some nefarious scheme against those financial pillars of the community.

Somehow, throughout all my trips to the bank, no towering bank officer or armed guard ever accosted me. But certainly I was scrupulously observed during these visits, especially when daring to go into the main banking room with the huge shining metal vault door, encased in solid granite and steel, staring down the center of the room like some all-seeing, all-knowing eye.

In all likelihood, I was probably more frightened by this sterile environment than impressed with the regal surroundings and executive royalty.

Aunt Lola performed some kind of clerical work and occasionally worked as a teller. Normally accompanied by some of my school chums, we would stop by after class to see her and to bum a nickel or a dime for some foolhardy treat.

Being her favorite and only nephew, she would always indulge my whims. I would also solicit a few pencils, small pads, rubber bands, and paper clips from around her desk, as these were important items to have for my occasional schoolwork and more frequent pet projects.

Women mostly worked in Aunt Lola's department and many of them wore caps with the traditional green visor, which seemed to denote the banking environment in those early days. These ladies were always friendly and welcomed me when entering their area looking for a financial donation from my aunt.

In my mind, she was one of the most important people in the bank. Married to my mother's brother, Russell, she had no children of her own, consequently she treated me like a son and endorsed my little whims with adoring enthusiasm.

My first real business encounter with a financial institution occurred upon opening a savings account in the tenth grade, while living with my father in Kannapolis, North Carolina, as my parents were then divorced.

Realizing the necessity to accumulate some savings for a "rainy day," I decided to put a little money together for my future needs by establishing my first bank account. The subsequent accumulation of funds in this new venture would have no material affect on the profitability or growth of the institution.

My Grandmother Lockhart, Della, on my mother's side of the family, taught me to be frugal. She preached in those early years the necessity of being thrifty, and frequently implored me to save half of any money that came into my possession.

That woman could stretch the value of a dollar better than any person I have ever known. She imbued a strong thrift mentality in me, which is still harbored today, much to the chagrin of my family members.

She and my Grandfather, Bert, had been farmers in West Virginia for most of their lives. In their latter years they lived on my grandfather's pension check, which resulted from his duty in the Army, as a member of Teddy Roosevelt's Rough Riders in Cuba, and later during the Spanish American War.

Somehow, she was able to carve out a decent living from that meager allotment and their farming activities during the forties and fifties. She was a wonderful financial manager and took great care to make certain everyone in the family had what they needed, regardless of the impact on her and my grandfather.

Each week I would visit the bank in this small North Carolina town and deposit my money to a passbook savings account. Banks were not computerized in those days; consequently, the teller would hand inscribe in black ink my deposited amount along with the current date in my highly prized and valuable small, green savings account book. My deposits would range from 50 cents to a dollar. Frequently, the book would be retrieved from its concealed location to allow me to view my growing largess.

It was always exciting when the extra benefit of quarterly interest was hand-posted in my passbook. This would require an extra visit to the bank to personally ensure a timely accounting. At the end of the twelve-month period, the accumulated funds were $100, resulting from a hundred or more visits to the bank to sequester my funds inside this financial monolith.

My diligence and dedication to the accumulation of wealth had paid off with this weighty sum. I was quite confident the bank tellers considered me a prime depositor and, of course, afforded all the respect befitting an important and "significant depositor."

No other banking involvement occurred until my enrollment in college, and another savings account was then opened for my summer earnings. These funds would quickly disappear by the fall, after school had started, which was probably common for most students.

My financial "ace in the hole" was a football scholarship at Marshall College that paid for most of my school expenses. Otherwise, without this invaluable monetary assistance, I would have been a destitute college student most of the time.

After four years of mostly being "force fed" a college education, while playing varsity football, basketball, and track, my graduation occurred in 1959 with the presentment of a Bachelor's Degree in Business Administration.

This academic achievement was not stellar by any standard, C+ grade average at best. But, I had made it through college in four years, while playing three sports and being an active member of the Pi Kappa Alpha fraternity.

My academic achievements, along with a pending military obligation, did not allow for many job entrees when the recruiters visited our campus. For these reasons I was summarily relegated to seeking low-paying employment opportunities, wherever they could be found.

My father's brother, Blakeney, lived at Ocean Drive Beach, South Carolina, which is now North Myrtle Beach. Upon graduation, he offered me a position with his small real estate firm, Jackson Realty, for the summer.

The job included renting and cleaning beach cottages, assisting with sales, and doing other odd jobs for $50 a week and room and board in their summer tourist home, Jackson Villa, which was located on the beach.

It was not a financially rewarding position, but the environment was fabulous. I learned something about real estate and insurance, but more importantly discovered some natural sales and people skills existed within my limited repertoire of ability. These attributes would be of significant benefit to me in my later occupations.

The summer was spent at the beach working and taking advantage of whatever female opportunities came my way. Ocean Drive was a favorite summer spot for visiting college students. It had a well-known, popular pub and dance hall called, "The Pad."

Their small band played all the great beach music of the day normally throughout the "wee" hours of the night.

Many late hours were spent there dancing the "shag" with the visiting college girls. For those too young to recall, the shag was a shuffling type of slow jitterbug dance. The young dancers appeared as if they were slowly gliding on sand around the dance floor. Actually, they were at Ocean Drive, because "The Pad" was only about 50 yards from the beach.

After the fun and frivolity of the summer months ended and all the students went back to school, it soon became apparent how lonely the beach could be without hordes of people around to socialize with.

By mid-September I began to go stir crazy with the emptiness, sand, never-ending waves, and rapidly approaching bleak wintry skies. The only activity seemed to be people fishing on the shoreline. To this day fishing does not appeal to me, because it seems so unexciting and dreary, most likely the result of my lonely perspective from that time.

My uncle had intimated he would be willing to take me on as a partner in his business in the near future. But, I couldn't see myself living in this semi-cloistered, partly uninhabited, and slow paced-environment during the long winter months of the year, under any circumstances.

Inside my psychic was a stirring and gnawing need for more excitement and stimulation than the beach could provide regularly. This was especially significant for someone my age, who had a lot of youthful "piss and vinegar" flowing through their veins.

The business proposition was declined and I departed in late October for Huntington in search of new opportunities, adventure, and most importantly, a job.

Throughout the summer many hours had been spent working-out on the beach running and exercising in anticipation of a tryout with the Baltimore Colts professional football team. The Colts had extended a free agent offer when I graduated from college.

As far back as my memory will now allow in my days as a young boy, running and playing games in our neighborhood, I had harbored the desire to play a professional sport and, of course, to be a star performer. Such are the dreams of the young and the regrets of the old.

After months of soul searching and concluding that this was not the best thing for me at this time in my life, I temporarily gave up on that dream. It was necessary to put my military service behind me, before I would be able to make any kind of commitment about a permanent job, a career, or sports.

In the early sixties, young, single men were required to serve either six months on active duty, followed by five and half years of reserve duty, or spend a total of three continuous years on active duty to fulfill their military obligation.

Many companies would not proffer a job opportunity to a single, male college student unless his obligation was fulfilled in one form or the other. Obviously, they were concerned about hiring people, who would shortly leave their organization after being trained and possibly not return upon completion of their military service.

The normal response of the corporate recruiter, prompted frequently during the employment interview, unless you were a student with superior credentials, which were not included in my dossier was, "Come back and see us when Uncle Sam is finished with you."

These were the conditions faced upon returning to Huntington in October 1959. In addition, due to a shortage of funds, it was necessary for me to move in with my mother, her husband, Jenks, and my grandfather at their home. This was not the most desirable of circumstances, but it was my only alternative.

Within a few weeks a position was obtained with a small local office of the Retail Credit Company, the forerunner of Equifax, as an insurance inspector with a salary of $250 a month and car expenses.

My investigation routine was primarily oriented to insurance claims, and it didn't take me long to realize this was not to be my life-long passion. After only a few months on the job, I decided to undertake my military obligation, otherwise, I would be in "Never-Never Land," floating aimlessly until that obligation was fulfilled.

The Marine Corps caught my fancy. They advertised on their recruiting posters; **"The Marine Corps Builds Men."** Its reputation as a rough and tough organization, and the highly publicized "macho" image they promoted when comparing the Marines to the other branches of the military strongly appealed to me.

Personally, it was necessary to do some more growing-up and the discipline, which was a Marine hallmark, would be beneficial to this maturation progress.

Also, I wanted to play football in the Marines. With the added age, physical growth, and experience the time in the Corps would be helpful, particularly if I chose to try-out for the professional ranks upon completion of my required three years of military service.

It was impossible to comprehend, upon joining the Corps, what I was about to put myself through physically and mentally. Also, it was not possible to foresee the future demands and responsibilities that those of us in the military services would have to shoulder over the next few years during a very difficult period in our country's history. It was called Vietnam.

I applied to take the Officers Candidate Test. In January, my orders arrived with instructions to report to Quantico, Virginia in March 1960 for admission to the 26th Officers Candidate Program. The Training and Test Regiment conducted this course at Marine Corps Schools in Quantico.

Departing Huntington in early March by train, I arrived the next morning at the large Marine base in Quantico and was on my way to becoming a Marine officer with all the traditions and history of this spirited military organization.

It would be quickly instilled in my mind that "Once a Marine always a Marine," was not just a trite saying, but an appropriate truism never to be forgotten or diminished in one's lifetime. Particularly, after proudly wearing the Corps "Globe and Anchor" insignia on your uniform for any length of time.

The decision to enter the Corps was perhaps the most important in my life up to that time. It would inexorably alter my destiny, validate my value system, provide structure to my thought process, and ultimately direct most of my future career choices.

It was the crucible that molded me into the kind of person I wanted to be. I was required to grow up, accept responsibility for my actions, never retreat from my commitments, and to always conquer my fears with courage. **Semper Fidelis--Always Faithful,** the Marine Corps slogan, would be indelibly etched into my sub-conscious for the rest of my life---not a bad thing.

Finally, the importance of honor, respect, and integrity were driven into my subconscious, like spikes in a granite wall, never to be loosened, but to hold fast in all relationships and responsibilities. This was the legacy bestowed on me and I have never deviated from it.

After joining the Corps in 1960, the next eight years would be spent as an active duty Marine officer, concluding in January 1968, after returning from duty in South Vietnam.

Initially, I was stationed for two years at Quantico attending various schools, coaching the Marine Corps Schools track team, and training officer candidates in the same type of program I had recently completed.

I participated in football and track for one season each. But, found my interests and my former athletic talents beginning to decline as my enthusiasm for this interesting and demanding career opportunity grew rapidly with each new exposure to the different aspects of military life.

My daughter, Kimberly, was born in December 1961 at the naval hospital in Quantico. A few months later, after being promoted to a First Lieutenant and completion of my assigned tour, we received a change of duty station orders.

In June 1962, I was directed to report to the Second Marine Division at Camp Lejeune, North Carolina and was assigned to the First Battalion, Eighth Marines as the executive officer of an infantry rifle company.

My son, Christopher, was born during our two years at Lejeune, at the base hospital, in November 1963.

Two years were spent training Marines with side excursions to Cuba for two months, during the Missile Crisis in October 1962, and deployment aboard ship in the Mediterranean Sea for the first six months of 1964.

Our battalion was the alert or standby unit for any worldwide type of emergency on October 18, 1962 when we were informed we were to be flown out that evening on troop transports to meet a developing contingency. Our ultimate destination was undisclosed until we were actually on the cargo airplanes in-flight to our objective, Guantanamo Bay, Cuba.

This was a critical time in the world, as Russia and the United States nearly went to war because of the missiles the Soviets had deployed on Cuban soil. Our President, John Kennedy, demanded they be removed and dispatched the Marines as a "show of force," and for potential defense of our Cuban Naval base in the event the Russians did not comply and war ensued.

Few people today realize just how close we came to a nuclear war over this situation. The tenuous controversy lasted for nearly two weeks until it was finally resolved when Russia agreed to remove the missiles demanded by our government. We vacated some bases in middle Europe, as a quid pro quo, in order to peacefully and politically solve this dilemma.

This was my first and closest exposure to war. We spent two months on the island of Cuba preparing defensive positions around our base for protection in the event of attack. After the crisis passed, we were transferred back to Camp Lejeune by ship in mid-December, just in time for Christmas.

Shortly after our return I was given the command of a Rifle Company and held that position for seven months. This was a significant leadership position, especially for a junior officer such as myself.

In January 1964 our reinforced infantry battalion departed the United States on Naval ships for the Mediterranean Sea. We would spend the next six months deployed as a Force in Readiness for war-type contingencies in that region of the world.

Our mission was to conduct amphibious operations on various islands, as training exercises, to ensure our combat readiness, and to be prepared to provide assistance to any friendly country in the event of hostilities.

We had one close call when a Greek and Cypriot war developed between the inhabitants on the island of Cyprus, just as we arrived on the scene. We were required to remain within 10 hours of sailing time of the island for a six-week period during this particular crisis. Our mission was to provide protection for U.S. government property and the potential evacuation of Americans, if either were threatened.

Fortunately, the situation was resolved and we continued in our peacekeeping and training role. In early May, we steamed for home, arriving some two weeks later, after the lengthy time away from our families.

In mid-summer of 1964 destiny arrived at my door in the form of a change-of-duty station orders. I was to be transferred to Oahu, Hawaii for assignment at Camp H. M. Smith, named after a famous and highly successful Marine General in the Second World War, "Howling Mad" Smith. The base was located in the hills, Aiea Heights, overlooking Pearl Harbor.

By then, nearly four years of service had been accumulated on active duty, as the result of accepting a regular commission upon completion of Basic School, a kind of officer's finishing class, in Quantico.

My required military service time was nearing completion, and my wife and I had seriously discussed leaving the Corps. We had been planning our next step since arriving home from my sojourn to the Mediterranean.

Upon receiving the unexpected change-of-station orders to Hawaii, we were perplexed about my next career decision. Should I go on with the plans and resign my commission or go to Hawaii and extend my time in the Marines?

No contacts had been made for a job outside the Corps. We finally reasoned this would probably be the only time we would visit that part of the world. So, the decision was made to extend my service obligation for at least two more years.

We knew Hawaii would be a wonderful place to live, and as a young couple with two small children we viewed this as an almost idyllic opportunity at this stage in our lives.

Our decision, to remain in the Marine Corps and relocate to Honolulu, would impact my destiny in a way no one could have foreseen at that time. This was truly a life defining choice, made in near desperation and confusion, because no other direction or course of action seemed plausible to us.

If the decision to leave the Corps had been made, it is impossible to determine what direction my life or career might have taken. However, one point is absolutely clear, I would not have gone to the war in Southeast Asia, which did occur some 24 months later, after making what seemed like a simple and reasonable decision to move my family to Hawaii.

So much for controlling one's destiny. But this was just the tip of the iceberg, so to speak. I would continue to direct my future and destiny in many situations in both the Marines and later in business, through my personal actions, judgements, and decisions without recognizing the impact to my life until much later.

It would be many years before realizing just how much direction I had, almost unconsciously, given to my life and career by these early decisions. But, this is the way a person influences his or her life, by choice and decisiveness.

My family departed for Honolulu by a military transport ship from San Francisco after driving across country in early August 1964. It was not a first-class experience, but it was fun and an interesting mode of travel. However, at the time we arrived on the beautiful island of Oahu, we were unaware of just how much the winds of that Asian war in Vietnam were increasing in momentum and the ultimate sacrifices that would impact so many young people.

Camp Smith, located on Oahu, was the senior Headquarters for both the Navy and Marine Corps Commands in the Pacific area, and was staffed with high-ranking officers from all branches of the military.

While stationed there much of my time was spent developing training programs and conducting weekend field tactical exercises for all enlisted Marines at the base.

As the war continued to expand into 1965, we directed the majority of our time and efforts on counter-guerrilla training. It was primarily based on "lessons learned" from combat reports received from the deployed Marine units in South Vietnam.

My interest in this warfare intensified and I began to study all the information published on the battle tactics of this war. It was a critical requirement to know how to defend against the unusual tactics employed by the Vietcong and North Vietnamese regular army troops.

Specifically, much of my attention was oriented to the enemy's use of booby traps and the plausible methods that could be employed to mitigate the devastation of our troops when they encountered these terrible weapons.

The booby trap device could take on many different forms and was probably responsible for more injuries and deaths in this war than any other single weapon used by the enemy. For me it was imperative to learn everything possible about them, so as to facilitate the use of counter-measures when my time came to fight in that devilish war.

During, 1965 I lobbied diligently through the command headquarters and my senior commanding officer for approval to attend the British Army jungle-warfare school, which was located north of Singapore in the heavily vegetated Malaysian jungle.

For a designated staff officer this was not normally authorized. But, because of my persistent efforts, pleading, cajoling, begging, selling, and promising to include the important issues learned into our training program upon returning, my Commanding Officer, Colonel A. D. Cherigino, finally acquiesced or hopelessly gave in, and allowed me to attend.

When the hidden voice in your subconscious talks to you about things you should do, listen carefully. It may just be some of the best advice you will ever hear.

Destiny was again preparing to affect my future as a result of this decision. From this unique training experience, which had literally been demanded by me in a polite way, of course, I would acquire skills and knowledge that would be of unbelievable help to my unit when we engaged the enemy in combat later in Vietnam.

After returning from the jungle training, the promise to my boss was fulfilled, and we incorporated much of those educational experiences from the course into our own syllabus.

Many senior officers at the base, who visited our creative and timely training exercises, said we probably would help save lives in Vietnam as the result of the current combat knowledge we imparted to these Marines.

Lieutenant General Victor Krulak, the Commanding General of all the Marine units in the Pacific Theatre, noted these achievements, when he presented a letter of commendation to me for our realistic training methods.

Interestingly, I learned a great deal about marketing from Krulak. He was a master at presenting and selling the Corps in a positive way at every opportunity.

Whenever the Marines in Hawaii conducted any kind of parade, ceremony, or demonstration for the public or other members of the armed forces, he required that it be a paragon of salesmanship, professionalism, and marketing of the Corps.

General Krulak, although small in size, a little over five feet tall, was nonetheless a whirling dervish as a commander and perfectionist when it came to planning, details, and timely job completion. And it always had to be accomplished in a highly professional manner.

He owned a distinguished battlefield reputation, and had previously served in the Kennedy administration as a staff officer and specialist on counter-guerrilla warfare during the early stages of the United States involvement in the war.

God help the staff officer who failed to submit well thought- out "white papers" on his assigned subject. Also, all work efforts had to conform to specific time schedules; otherwise, the General's wrath would spew forth in a threatening manner causing a major upheaval among his staff.

Perhaps it was from my close observation of General Krulak and his methods, along with my training, experiences in Vietnam, and the emphasis placed on fulfilling your mission that taught me one of my most important management and leadership rules, which I have taken some liberty with to paraphrase.

Do what you say you're going to do and do it when you say you're gonna to do it. People are counting on you. No excuses will be tolerated and failure is not acceptable.

Not a bad axiom for the military or private industry. It's too bad more managers and companies don't preach and practice this personal and corporate commitment on a regular basis.

Many say the Marine Corps has the best advertising and propaganda program of any organization in the world. The Corps has been able to create a top-of-mind awareness to the public over the years that is second to none. They sell a kind of mystique about manhood, toughness, dedication to country and patriotism, which most people acknowledge and can identify with, regardless of their background or beliefs.

They sold me hook, line, and sinker for eight years. Actually, I have never really departed from that mindset, much to the chagrin of some of my business associates.

After one year in Hawaii, I decided to continue with a military career. Toward the end of my second year, after some very serious soul searching, I requested a transfer to Vietnam. My goal was to command an infantry rifle company in combat.

Within three months a positive response to my request arrived. It was important to climb that mountain and meet my destiny; otherwise, I could never claim to be a professional warrior. In my mind this was required and it had to be done. There was no other way.

In the summer of 1966 my family was relocated to Charlotte, North Carolina, and a few weeks later I was on a military aircraft heading back to California. After 30 days of preliminary combat training at Camp Pendleton, I was on my way "In Country."

It would be there at Pendleton, during instruction on the enemy employment of booby traps that another opportunity to influence my destiny occurred.

Always take advantage of every educational opportunity,

it will enhance your career, or it might just save your life.

A mock booby-trap course, simulating the types of devices and clandestine ways they were used by the enemy in Vietnam, particularly concealed along trails and paths for the unsuspecting foot soldier on patrol, was included in the training regimen.

Because of my extreme interest in this specific warfare technique, I decided to spend more than my allotted time learning how to locate and disarm them. After several hours walking the trails, trying to hone my attention and skills, I finally concluded the indoctrination when darkness overtook me. All of the other troops had long departed for more stimulating leisure activities. However, my persistence and near blind determination would pay enormous dividends in the very near future.

Four months later, while on a combat patrol with my rifle company in South Vietnam, I stepped on a trip wire, which was connected to a booby-trapped white phosphorus grenade. The pressure from my foot on the wire had pulled the safety pen from the device and armed it for detonation.

My radio operator and I were walking together on a trail leading into a small Vietnamese village during a search and destroy mission. We were adjacent to some of our troops, moving cautiously on a separate path while we looked for signs of the Vietcong in the immediate vicinity. Suddenly, detecting an almost inaudible click, without thinking I immediately glanced down to the ground and recognized a small, almost invisible, monofilament string or fishing line under the toe of my boot. The weight of my foot and pressure on the tripwire had triggered and armed the booby trap.

Without hesitation and certainly no "paralysis through analysis," I grabbed my radio operator, who was just a step behind me, pushed him violently, and screamed "run!"

We bolted away just seconds before the explosion, covering about 10 yards in record time, just as the molten jelly spewed forth from the grenade in all directions.

My radio operator was hit by a small piece of the burning substance on his leg, and the hot phosphorus luckily only struck my protective flak jacket and canteen.

Fortunately, we were able to arrest the burning gelatin on his thigh by smothering it with dirt. This stopped the airflow that feeds the fuel. After some minor first aid treatment he was able to continue on the mission. I had to throw the canteen away, it was ruined, but continued wearing my 14-pound flak jacket and was damned glad to have had it on my body that day.

Many nights we slept in those heavy padded jackets for extra protection from any flying shrapnel resulting from surprised enemy artillery or mortar attacks.

The extra training conducted on that long afternoon at Camp Pendelton and the resultant heightened sensitivity it produced to these devices had resulted in saving both our lives. Many times I have thought about the possible consequences of the event. What if I had left that training early, as did most of the men at the end of the day, and gone to the club for a more relaxing time and a beer?

In all probability, without that extra time practicing on the course, it is likely we would not have survived the incident.

As a result of these kinds of experiences I have continually emphasized training for my staff and employees at every opportunity. I was able to benefit from the value of my training experiences by staying alive and by helping my men to stay out of Harm's Way.

In addition, the training received at the British Army Jungle Warfare School in Malaysia was also important and helpful. Many of the combat techniques taught during that course were used in their entirety or modified to meet the unusual tactics employed by our enemy.

Conventional thinking was not the way to win in Vietnam. It was necessary to continually develop new techniques, employ creative tactics, out-think or think-like your enemy and anticipate the next move. It was product development and strategy formulation on the run. The same rules apply in business, if you want to beat the competition.

Our search and destroy tactics was altered by varying our methods of troop deployment, attack methodology, and the use of the element of surprise when pursuing the enemy.

We developed a probing device called the "Mike Spike," (named for our company), to locate underground hiding places and tunnels. We also developed another device to help uncover the tunnel entrance and detonate hidden explosives without exposing our men to the blast effects.

These same instruments, especially the probe, were also of great help to our troops in locating concealed booby traps, weapons and supplies. Our tactics and makeshift devices gave us an advantage in our battle zone and significantly reduced the potential injury to our troops from the enemy's machinations.

To my knowledge, no other military unit exploited their aggressors with the same type of tactics that we employed in our specific area of operations.

We won "our little war" in our tactical area and the results of our conflicts, which were documented and promulgated through various military communications, clearly identified our successes.

These unique methods, creative fighting techniques and unconventional warfare tactics also received recognition in the Armed Forces Stars and Stripes newspaper.

Additionally, the Commanding Officer of the Third Marine Division, Major General Kyle, also noted our achievements when he dispatched the following message to us and copied all units in the Division:

"The excellent results obtained by Mike company 3/4 in aggressive search and destroy missions have been noted with pleasure. Indicative of excellent combat leadership and high-level troop proficiency has been the capture/kill of numerous VC, the location of arms and equipment, and the uncovering of tunnels and caches. Keep up the good work."

The point was; we got more of the enemy than they got of us and that's the way the score was kept.

Toward the conclusion of my 13-month tour, I became disgusted and worn-out with the war like so many other Americans, and reluctantly decided to resign my commission at the end of my tour of duty.

My personal goals had been accomplished during the time in the Marines, and fortunately my combat command time had been successful. Our unit had suffered limited casualties during the combat action, and with God's guidance, most of us were coming home alive and in one-piece.

It was time to move on and find another occupation at age 31. After submitting my letter of resignation, upon being selected for promotion to major, my discharge occurred after arriving home from Vietnam in January 1968.

During the last few months overseas I had taken the Graduate Record Exam with the aspiration to attend graduate school. Also, over 100 letters were written and mailed to various companies soliciting their interest and a job interview.

No inquiries were sent to any bank or financial services organization for obvious reasons. In my mind I just didn't seem to fit the mold or possess the requisite financial background.

After leaving Vietnam, it was learned my scores on the examination were not satisfactory and would require a successful re-test in order to qualify for graduate school. Also, my corporate job inquiry correspondence attracted no more than four interested responses.

Deciding to forgo my thinking about school, my only recourse was to seek immediate employment. There were no financial resources or family wealth to help me through any elapsed time period. With a wife and two small "curtain climbers" (Marine term for children) to feed after leaving the government payroll, it was necessary to make a quick decision and get on with a job search.

Arriving home in mid-December the interviewing process began immediately with concentration on those few companies that had responded favorably to my earlier letters.

After the interviews were completed, I finally accepted a position with Boise Cascade in one of their new fiberboard manufacturing plants located in West Memphis, Arkansas.

In late January, we sold the house in Charlotte, packed our belongings in our only automobile, and full of hopes and dreams, headed toward a new start in life.

With my Marine Corps career behind me and optimistic about the future, but uncertain as to the methods and actions needed to achieve success in the business world, I was nevertheless mentally prepared to direct all of my efforts toward this new undeveloped opportunity.

Looking back on these years now, the decision to join the Corps and become an officer was absolutely perfectly timed for me at that critical point in my life. Those were important and impressionable years for a young man trying to define himself.

The depth of my military education, exposure to many varied situations and trying experiences provided the nucleus and confidence to undertake a new quest in life.

But, for the immediate future it was necessary to experience a personal set-back with my first job in the "civilian world," in order to gain the insight on the type of work that was most suitable for me.

Sorting through many personal issues on this initial job and discovering the wrong employment decision had been made; destiny again intervened in my life and delivered me at the doorstep of the banking world.

However, the ultimate decision on the course of action to take was left for me to make. And that's the way it's supposed to work.

If you keep trying, regardless of the obstacles or misdirected efforts, one usually ends up in the right place. This seems to be an immutable fact and makes a sustainable point that you should never, never, never, give in to adversity. It should be viewed only as providing another opportunity to learn and excel.

Chapter Three
The First National Bank of Atlanta

Upon our arrival in Memphis in January 1968, we located a small-furnished apartment in the White Haven area, about two miles from Graceland, the home of Elvis Presley. Many Sundays we would see him in the large fenced yard in front of his home riding horses would later tell my friends we were his neighbors, just a little exaggeration on my part.

I reported to work at the fiberboard plant, which was located in West Memphis, Arkansas, across the wide Mississippi River, and started my training program with the company.

It didn't take long for me to realize the wrong decision had been made with my initial job selection, even though Boise Cascade was a fine company and growing rapidly.

It was difficult grasping the rudiments of scheduling and operating certain types of machinery. In addition, the confinement of working in the bowels of a manufacturing facility day in and day out with little access to the outside world was disconcerting. There was no excitement, except for the noise of the equipment, and absolutely no adventure to stir the internal juices.

Deciding a change was critical to my survival, I started looking for a new job within a few weeks, eventually locating a position advertised in the local Memphis newspaper, and was ultimately offered employment with The First National Bank of Atlanta. We moved there after a period of only six weeks in Memphis.

I had initially flown into Atlanta from Vietnam to meet my wife and get reacquainted after our 14-month separation. After three months, including my job search, a relocation to Memphis from Charlotte, and several weeks in a manufacturing position, we were now back in Atlanta seeking to start our new life the second time with another company. My employment started at First National on March 4, 1968.

The banking environment was quite competitive in Atlanta in the sixties. First National and Citizens and Southern National Bank were the largest banks in the city. Trust Company Bank, which had a major holding of Coca-Cola stock in its investment portfolio was the third largest, followed by a number of smaller institutions, including Fulton National and the National Bank of Georgia. All of these institutions had branches scattered throughout the metropolitan area.

Also, a number of savings and & loan institutions, including Georgia Federal, a Federal Savings Bank, my future employer, were located in the city.

Mills B. Lane, who headed Citizens and Southern and James Robinson, Chairman of First National, were the two major and most well known bankers in the state. Mr. Lane was famous for wearing a bright tie with the inscription "It's a wonderful world," prominently displayed down the front.

Mr. Robinson, a physically large man, was not as flamboyant, but both men were aggressive bankers and active participants and contributors in the early development of Atlanta. Ivan Allen was the mayor at that time and was very progressive with his growth programs for the city. He was extremely popular with all factions in Atlanta.

Mr. Robinson passed away shortly before I joined the bank and was replaced by Edward D. Smith, an attorney by education. Mr. Smith was a good businessman and followed in Robinson's footsteps by introducing new products and services to promote the growth of the bank.

Statewide branching was not permitted in Georgia at this time, although some of the larger institutions had an ownership position in a few small banks around the state that were "grandfathered," because their ownership position predated the current law.

The failure of the Georgia state legislature to change this confining non-branching legislation, until some years later, was the principal reason banks grew more rapidly in a few of the neighboring states, primarily North Carolina, which was more liberal with their branching and acquisition regulations. Ultimately, these banks in the "Tarheel" state became financially dominant, because of their flexible banking laws and eventually purchased many of the institutions in Georgia.

Most banking institutions were primarily involved in providing only traditional financial services.

By the late sixties, many banks in the state were beginning to form bank holding companies. These new organizations would ultimately provide the vehicle for the bankers to broaden the types of financial products they could offer in their markets. The corporate structure would also facilitate the purchase of additional banks and statewide branching, when the bank regulations were later amended.

The descriptive term used for bank holding companies was "congeneric," meaning that all owned subsidiaries were principally related to the financial services sector.

In the early eighties, branching was allowed in contiguous counties and states, but by that time our out-of-state competitors were already beginning to surpass the Georgia banks in the growth of assets through the acquisition process. This enhanced their future capability to acquire even more institutions and integrate them into their growing franchise.

As history clearly reflects, because of the more liberal banking laws in the other states, most of the large banks in Atlanta were acquired, leaving only Trust Company, now Sun Trust Banks, as the largest Atlanta home-based financial institution currently in existence in the city.

First National Bank was located on the corner at Five Points, so-named because five streets converged in the downtown area on the famous Peachtree Street, which was also the major and most well-known thoroughfare in Atlanta.

A new 41-story building was under construction and was nearly completed when I joined the company. Both the adjacent old six-story building and the new super-structure were joined together in the construction process and the resultant First National Tower would become, temporarily, the tallest building in the city.

First National had $1.5 billion in assets. Under today's standards it would be considered a medium-size institution.

Bank of America, located in San Francisco, was the largest bank in the United States with about $20 billion in assets. Today, the largest financial institutions have well in excess of $400 billion in assets.

The number of banks and savings and loans approached 20,000 collectively, not including branches. Many pundits of the industry thought we were over-banked in the United States.

Consolidation of financial organizations had been underway in many foreign countries for several years. Consequently, there were fewer banks, with more branches, and much larger asset bases than existed in America.

The United States banking community would ultimately pursue this same consolidation process, creating some mega-sized institutions in this country. But, even with this mentality in play for the past several years, there are still more banks in the U.S. than any other country.

My former employer, First National, was eventually purchased by Wachovia Bank in Winston Salem, North Carolina. In 2002, First Union Corporation, based in Charlotte, merged with Wachovia creating a $400 billion organization.

First National was in the process of offering a new revolutionary service in 1968. It was a credit card licensed through The North Carolina National Bank in Charlotte. Now, it is called The Bank of America. The card was BANCAMERICARD, which is now known as VISA.

Credit cards were just beginning to enter the market, on a small scale and only one bank provided a card in Georgia. Citizens and Southern (C&S) offered a limited-distribution proprietary card for their customers, which was only accepted in Georgia at select C&S customer merchant locations.

First National conducted a major kick-off campaign in and around Atlanta, utilizing over 100 sales people from the company to solicit merchant participants, while mailing cards to a large base of consumers. I was a member of the merchant sales group, and would spend my first two months calling on retail prospects.

Needless to say, the program was successful, and the bank far exceeded both its merchant and cardholder acceptance expectations for this introductory card. This was a major product offering of the time, and credit cards would soon become one of the most widely used financial products in the history of banking.

Today, can you imagine not having use of one or more of these ubiquitous cards when you are shopping or traveling? Prior to the introduction of the credit card, all transactions were primarily by cash, check, or charged to the customers' account. These transaction methods although still prominent, seem archaic compared to the world of credit card purchasing activity today.

Banking has been a leader in the installation and utilization of computer technology, because of its need to process large amounts of data, checks, and other various customer transactions.

The smaller community banks, as a result of the costs associated with this technology, normally contracted for their computer services with the larger institutions or their primary correspondent banks. These institutions provided them with multiple types of banking assistance, including loan participations and general funding services.

A few large banks installed data processing centers in the smaller, more distant cities, where their customer banks were located, for convenience purposes. The user banks, normally much smaller in asset size could transport their checks and other accounting needs to these centers at the close of business for processing, thereby ensuring overnight turnaround of the work.

The computer centers would assimilate the data and then transmit it via high-speed telephone lines to their primary computer operations center at the host institution where the mainframe high-speed processing equipment was located. After the updates had been completed, reports would be transmitted back over-night to the remote computer center, printed, and delivered early the next morning by land courier to the customer bank.

First National did not operate any of these centers, when I joined the company, but they were on the future-planning horizon.

The bank had a large IBM 360 system installed on the fourth floor in its headquarters building, where all in-house processing was conducted. The 360 system was only a couple of years old, but technology was changing so rapidly it would be replaced shortly by a new, faster, and more capable machine, the IBM 155.

As time progressed, in the maturation process of computer technology, all machines would become more proficient, faster, and require less physical space due to the improved circuitry and other related technology.

In essence, the machines were becoming more powerful and capable of handling multiple tasks, while simultaneously requiring less space for storage and operation.

While learning about this dynamic new business tool in the late sixties, an article was noted in a technology magazine containing a quote that seemed to define the status and the future prospects of the industry. It read, "The computer industry, after growing wildly for the past twenty years, is now finally reaching infancy."

It would be interesting, maybe impossible to describe the last thirty years of technology enhancements since the article was written. The overwhelming and far-reaching advances of the computer field have impacted and invaded nearly every aspect of our lives and everything we do in our work and leisure activities.

My first management position, after heading a team for two months to install an IBM model-20 card system for a trust application, was to manage the data preparation department.

In those early days, much of the information from original documents was punched into cards by operators using keypunch machines, and then input by card readers into the computer system for processing.

Information created from these documents was usually stored on magnetic disk or tape units for future use. Afterwards, both could be read or written on by the computer systems at high speed, but the initial input information was frequently supplied in the now archaic card format.

Many of the computer departments worked around the clock, six to seven days a week, because of the scheduling constraints and demands of the user. In the keypunch or data entry department, many of the employees were women. They worked on production standards and were paid a bonus based on the amount of data punched into the cards hourly.

Our management engineers department was staffed mostly with very bright Georgia Tech graduates, and was responsible for developing these standards. This was the type of job I had initially called about when seeking an interview in Memphis. Many of the backroom operating departments had standards developed for production and incentive wages, which would be the normal operating procedure in the future for most companies.

The biggest challenge was to keep our employees' morale high to ensure that the production and quality levels were maintained according to the job standards. This was a constant challenge, especially with the routine, sedentary, and repetitive nature of the work.

It was important to listen with undivided attention when various grievances, some major, many minor, were presented. Many times I found just listening with sympathetic understanding was enough to solve the problem, both those that were real and those imagined.

There seemed to be more morale and general personnel problems on the night shift, which is probably normal due to the nocturnal nature of the work and the small amount of outside attention generally provided during these hours. It was important to visit the staff on these late shifts frequently to show interest in their work, afford general attention, and provide kudos for a job well done.

We would present all the women in the keypunch department with a rose in a small vase and a thank you note to demonstrate our appreciation for their dedication and hard work.

Weekly "give and take" briefings and "atta girl" awards were also presented to ensure a continuous flow of communication and recognition.

The personal attention given to this department of 100 women helped maintain motivation, interest in their jobs, and on the team, while maintaining solid production results.

They cared about their work; because it was obvious their management and supervisors cared, openly demonstrated appreciation for their efforts, and personally recognized their results.

Sounds simple, but why don't more managers do it? Because they don't have time, don't know better, or just don't have the energy to make the effort.

I have always been amazed by the apathy many organizations openly displayed about employee motivation, particularly in today's business environment. With the earning and performance stresses put on many organizations it would seem that this important facet of management would be one of the top priorities in every company.

It's surprising how few managers really don't understand the significance or importance of basic courtesies. And how a simple "thank you" for a good job can enhance individual performance. I've always believed those two little words were some of the best and most effective motivators that any leader or manager could employ.

Constant communication and recognition are critical adjuncts to the success of any organization. Without emphasizing them regularly, how can any company hope to achieve their goals?

In the Marines this was very basic stuff and we referred to it as **Leadership 101.** The Marine Corps taught us that a leader has two primary objectives: **"To accomplish the mission and to take good care of your people."** I have never forgotten this simple, but significant leadership principal.

The same management tenets should be applicable in business and could be called **Elementary Management 101.**

During this time frame, Duane Hoover, the senior operations executive of the bank, who had initially interviewed and hired me, resigned from the bank to begin a new career in real estate.

Duane was a very bright and dynamic individual. I hated to see him leave the company, but he had greater opportunities apparently available to him than could be provided by First National.

After he departed, the operations division was divided into two separate groups. My new boss for the computer operations department was Forest Waddle, a long time employee of the bank from Kentucky, who had acquired a vast background in bank operations from his many years at the bank.

Roger White, who had also reported to Duane and was highly respected in the bank and by his peers in the other Atlanta institutions, assumed responsibility for the check processing area. He had also been with First National for many years and was considered to be one of the most knowledgeable bank operations executives in the country.

Not long after these changes, a number of other senior management positions opened up as a result of some senior management power conflicts in the bank. The issues were far over my head as a very junior officer. However, I seem to recall they were mostly "turf related."

While the struggles were underway one of my associates gave me some good advice. He said, "Just do your job, stay out of the line of fire (I learned that in Vietnam), and smile at everyone until the dust had cleared and someone was put in charge."

Winston Churchill, the former British Prime Minister of Great Britain, when asked about the dangers he faced in combat during his experiences in the Boer War offered an interesting observation when he said: "Bullets that fly over your head don't hurt."

His comment is applicable for most struggles, don't you think?

When the dust and battles finally settled, I had another new boss, Ben Rawlins, who had formerly been in charge of the programming department.

Ben, a graduate of Vanderbilt University, was very intelligent, quite business savvy, and dealt with me in a forthright manner. We became a good team and I developed a tremendous amount of respect for his management style and knowledge. He placed me in charge of all bank computer operations, and promoted me to a second vice president position with a nice pay raise. He definitely knew how to get people on his team.

Ben would later join Union Planters Bank, in Memphis and subsequently became Chairman and CEO. He did a great job building that organization into a large, profitable, regional banking company.

The new Computer Division was placed organizationally under the Money Management Department of the bank, which was headed by Bill Matthews. Bill eventually became President of the holding company, but left some time later when he was offered the CEO position at Union Planters Bank. Ben would ultimately follow him in that role a few years later.

Matthews departed the company after Tom Williams was hired as the obvious heir apparent to Mr. Smith.

Smith was motivated to bring in his own man to run the bank, who would eventually replace him when he retired. The logical assumption centered on his obvious belief that none of the current management executives had the requisite talent to fill his shoes.

Tom Williams moved to Atlanta from a bank in Cleveland, where he had been an executive vice president, after being personally recruited by Ed Smith. He became Chairman and Chief Executive of the entire company when Smith retired and held those positions for a number of years.

He stepped aside and retired after Wachovia Bank, located in Winston Salem, North Carolina, acquired First National.

Raymond Riddle, who had also held a number of different management positions in the company throughout his long tenure with the bank, became president under Williams. He would stay on as the head of the Georgia operations for Wachovia until he retired in the early-nineties, and later became the CEO of National Services, Inc. in Atlanta.

Andy Huber was another high-powered senior executive, who was caught up the management changes at the bank. He was a dynamic individual, who had married the daughter of the former Chairman of the company, Jim Robinson.

Andy was in charge of one of the largest divisions in the bank, and like Bill Matthews, had hoped to be designated as the new CEO of the company upon Smith's retirement.

This was not to be for either of these talented men. As a result, both eventually left FNB and chose other career routes more in line with their personal objectives.

After leaving First National, Andy joined another banking organization, Georgia Railroad and Banking Company, based in Augusta, and assisted in forming a new bank holding company in Atlanta, First Georgia Bancshares, a public company that owned First Georgia Bank, my future employer. Georgia Railroad had a 5% ownership interest in

First Georgia. The Railroad bank, as it was frequently called, had plans to use this ownership position to branch into Atlanta when the banking laws permitted.

Carl Sanders, the former governor of Georgia in the early sixties and now principal of a major law firm in Atlanta, Troutman, Sanders, Lockerman and Ashmore, was the most influential member of the board of First Georgia Bank. He was also a major stockholder in the Georgia Railroad Bank.

Huber served as chairman of the Bancshares Holding Company and the bank. He would remain in those positions for only a short time. Ultimately, he departed because of disagreement with the owners and directors concerning the operations and financial performance of the company. He eventually headed a Southeast regional banking office in Atlanta for Bank of America.

Similar management wars, like the one at First National, were probably occurring in other financial institutions in Atlanta at the same time. However, we were so caught up in our own skirmishes and personal survival that we didn't have the interest or desire to keep up with the schemes in the other bank conflicts.

In 1974, after being recruited by Sanders for the executive vice president position of First Georgia Bank, within four months the board elected me President and CEO of the Bank and the holding company, because of the financial problems in the company.

Huber was long gone and I had one huge mess on my hands to clean up. It would be a challenge and an opportunity that was almost too convoluted and messy for anyone to undertake, including a professional, who had extensive experience and problem bank workout knowledge.

After seven years in the industry I was nothing more than a neophyte in the banking world. Fortunately, I was not knowledgeable enough to understand the depth of the problems or the seriousness of the bank's financial condition. This probably inured to my benefit, because I didn't fully realize how impossible the situation was.

Destiny certainly had a role in mind for me in the Atlanta banking market, or so it seemed. Apparently, I was the only person around who would undertake such a fool-hearty task and attempt to salvage a basically "failed" financial institution---so the job was mine.

In early 1970, a decision was finally made at First National to broaden our share of the data processing services banking market in Georgia. It was decided we should locate remote computer centers in key cities to extend our capability and facilitate the growth opportunity of this business. The computer division would have the responsibility for implementation and management of these operations.

Over the next two years we installed computer centers in six markets, substantially improving our competitive position in this business. It was not an easy task, as many of our in-house software systems needed modification to support the centers and function in a multi-bank environment.

This was a complex programming task, especially for the primitive software applications of this time, requiring a large expenditure of time and resources.

New computer equipment, including check readers, sorters, data input devices, and high-speed telephone lines were installed in the centers to process the expected volumes and meet the critical turnaround times.

We conducted sales promotion events in all the major cities in Georgia and invited bankers from throughout the state to attend.

My role was to manage the operations and to make the sales presentations to the various banking prospects to explain our operation.

Product reception was very good. Our new technology and service capability would soon prove to be an idea and a need whose time had come.

We pinned a slogan, of sorts, on our product package, which seemed to satisfy all the factions in the bank, who believed they had an interest in the results of the business: "Providing tomorrow's services today." It was thought to be a creative phrase in those days.

First National received favorable press in various industry publications for our state-of-the-art operation. These centers produced good profits for the bank and resulted in a substantial increase in business.

Automated Teller Machines (ATM) were just coming into their own by 1970, with only a few thousand installed nationwide. First National launched one of the most successful ATM systems and marketing programs in the banking industry when "Tillie the Teller" was introduced.

The bank, with its introductory marketing program, presented the machine with an almost human identity in their advertising. It featured a real life perky young woman in a red and white pokka-dot dress identified as "Tillie the Teller." This approach was uniquely designed to provide the appearance of the machine as being highly user-friendly. The advertising promotion worked, by bringing new customers to the bank, and received national acclaim in several banking publications.

No other bank in the state of Georgia had installed an ATM system of any significance at the time. Actually, few banks nationwide held claim to a large distribution of these machines at the time of our introduction.

Today, the ATM is probably the single most used physical service device in the banking industry utilized to facilitate transactions for the customer throughout the world. Many of us have used our banking card to withdraw funds from a machine in a foreign country, in our own hometown at a branch, or perhaps in a stand-alone location at a shopping center or office building in a city where we are visiting.

The rhetorical question asked by many bankers, after the machines became so popular was, "now that we have trained the customer not to come into the bank to transact business, how in the world are we going to sell them any new products in the future?" It was a proper question at the time, because most bank product selling was done at the desk of the new account representative inside the branch.

Today, the banking industry has partially solved that problem by using more sophisticated selling techniques, including direct mail and Internet access to peddle their services.

However, face-to-face personal contact is absolutely the best method to sell products. Therein lies one of the largest challenges for automation. The younger, more technically oriented, fast paced customer of today and the future will easily migrate to these more fluid and less personal transaction modes.

The Automated Teller Machine is here to stay, and with the addition of new technology enhancements and service options it will become even more pervasive in the marketplace. Both the bank, as a result of lower operating costs, and the customer from convenience, pricing, and servicing capability will continue to be beneficiaries from this enhanced product offering.

Another service creating attention in the corporate marketplace in the early seventies was Cash Management.

Our National Corporate Lending Division, headed by Jack Dempsey, a senior vice president, believed his department needed this product to compete in the large National corporate market against the other major financial institutions.

The problem was that no one in the bank could adequately define the types of services and functions required, or how they should be marketed to the large corporate business customers.

Fortunately, the bank provided a number of both automated and labor-intensive processing services, which would ultimately become pieces of the so-called family of cash management products. These services would provide the foundation for the eventual development of our cash management package.

First National offered Lock Box processing, which was the receipt of bill payments of a client at a post office box in Atlanta, managed by the bank, that were mailed from various corporate customer locations in the Southeast. The payments were reconciled to the bills, copies made for the customer, and the checks immediately routed or sent to the bank they were drawn against for collection and immediate deposit to the client's account.

Since the checks and bill payments came from locations in the southern or eastern part of the United States, we would naturally receive them faster, because of our location and good mail service.

This process was much faster compared to payments being mailed to more distant locations of the company, and then deposited at remote banks, requiring further transfers until the money reached the principal bank of the company. This step extended the time before the funds became available, and ultimately impacted the time value of money.

Most of the banks, upon which the checks were drawn, were located in proximity to First National in the southeast, as was the Atlanta based Sixth District Federal Reserve Bank. Utilizing the Fed check collection system, First National could deposit and collect the checks faster from those banks in the Southeast where the accounts were maintained.

The extra time derived from the rapid deposit and collection of funds allowed the customer to begin drawing interest on these deposits more quickly than would have been the case without the use of the lock box service. Many times, depending on the size of the customer's receivables, the extra financial benefit derived from the faster collection process could result in millions of dollars of financial benefit.

The term used in the banking industry to define uncollected funds, money in-transit, not debited/credited, but is in the process of being collected and posted as usable funds is called "float."

At one time, in our recent history, the Federal Reserve System had prophesized uncollected funds would be severally reduced with the improved technology and processes in the check collection system. This has not yet been achieved in our rapidly growing and changing economy.

Float still exists and is an important part of the check writing process for many bank customers.

Both individuals and companies write checks on uncollected funds in anticipation deposits will be made prior to the time the check actually clears or is debited from their account balance. It is called, "playing the float," when checks are written prior to the actual deposit of the funds, and is a way of life in the banking world, although supposedly illegal.

Considering the millions or billions of dollars that pass through corporate accounts in normal transaction activity, and the potential opportunity costs derived from those funds if deposited and collected quickly, most large companies knew they could materially enhance their investment profitability when using cash management products.

Lock box processing was certainly a major piece of the cash management product line, but there were more "bells and whistles" needed to improve its effectiveness for the customer.

The concept behind an effective cash management program revolved around the rapid deposit of accounts receivable, immediate investment of those funds, quick reporting of financial information followed by the reconcilement of all check transactions. It also included the ability to rapidly transfer collected funds to a major disbursing account to meet the customer's needs.

A zero-balance checking account was also essential and provided the customer with a more precise method to track funds flow, by type, from those accounts.

All collected funds were deposited to the appropriate subsidiary account or zero-balance account. Disbursements were then made from these accounts and any remaining balances were automatically transferred to the master account at the end of the daily cycle. All excess funds, including funds for checks issued, but not yet debited from the customer's account, were invested for specified periods, usually overnight.

Zero-balance accounts provided an audit trail on both check issuing and deposit activity by consolidating usable balances into a single account. These accounts made it much easier for the client to determine the amount of unused funds available for overnight investment.

Reconcilement of the checking accounts was another ancillary cash management service necessary to close the funds tracking process and mitigate the internal labor costs of the customer. The checks written and paid were analyzed and reports provided by the bank to enable the customer to easily maintain his records of all check payment activity.

First Atlanta had some of these products, but they were not packaged in a way to derive maximum benefit for the user.

After much deliberation on how to proceed to develop a cash management program, management asked me to study the problem, attempt to find a solution, and provide it to the National Corporate Lending Division for their consideration.

Because of my operational background and familiarity with most of the transaction type products we currently provided, my name was thrown into the "discovery" pot. The challenge was to package the services in a way they could be integrated and presented logically to the customer, and to determine any new products that would be required to complete the system.

None of the senior executives seemed to have any idea how to do this without conducting a very time-consuming and expensive analysis. The timing for the introduction in the market seemed to be the most critical element.

After careful study, over a period of several weeks, a solution was presented to management. It was called "The Integrated Cash Management System."

The resultant package included several different collection type services to gather funds, multiple methods of disbursement of these monies, and finally a number of ways to provide the necessary management information to the customer on a regular basis in any format and communication channel.

The system was diagramed in a flow-chart model, explanations inserted on each product and the resulting diagram was packaged in a professional looking sales brochure for simplification to make it plausible to the customer and simple for our sales representatives to present.

Everyone liked the concept. Our systems people thought they could modify our current software to deliver the new additions. The National division believed it would serve their needs in the market. The pressure was lifted from the shoulders of several key executives, who were under some amount of professional stress, while vainly searching for an answer.

The next challenge was to take it on the road and present it to a few customers in its rudimentary format and obtain feedback.

Because of my involvement in the development of the "thing," I was chosen unilaterally to make the sales calls and initial presentations. Our corporate calling officers, who knew or understood very little about the products or how they worked, which was to be expected because they were primarily lending oriented, would accompany me and make the necessary introductions.

As a junior officer of the bank my status was considered expendable. It was like being one of the earliest Christians, who faced the hungriest lions.

The test presentations were made in Chicago to a few executives, at large corporations, who were knowledgeable on the subject and had corporate relationships with our bank.

Over a two-day period, 10 exhaustive presentations were made to corporate treasurers and comptrollers to determine if the system would meet their cash management needs.

The reception was overwhelmingly positive and each company responded favorably to our "in process" concept. The executives told us they had not seen any cash management system so well defined by a financial institution.

We had a winner. Now we had to complete the product, consolidate the services, and finalize our product introduction.

It was decided we would host a series of one-day sales seminars in key cities across the country and invite corporate financial executives from companies that seemed to have a need for the product.

This was a perfect sales platform to launch our new service. No other financial institution was using a similar sales approach, and we intended to maximize our opportunity.

The responsibility fell to me to establish a cash management department, coordinate presentations, and handle implementation when a sale occurred.

Over the next two years, we made monthly sales presentations to 2,500 executives in most of the large cities in America. The innovative marketing approach worked and we were phenomenally successful in adding new business over the following years.

There were few banks that could compete with us. However, Mellon Bank in Pittsburgh with Craig Ford, who was perhaps the most knowledge in the banking arena driving their business model, was recognized as the best in the cash management field. Continental Bank in Chicago and North Carolina National Bank in Charlotte were also considered to have strong positions, but none of these banks sold their product like First National Bank.

As a result of my exposure and involvement, I was selected, along with two other bankers, to join the U.S. Postal Services Cash Management Banking Advisory Committee. Our mission was to advise and help them develop additional tools similar to those used by other aggressive cash-minded corporations.

This occurred at the time the Postal Service became a privately operated organization and was in the process of consolidating a number of their post office banking accounts around the country to lower costs and improve profitability.

They were establishing a cash concentration system, through the Atlanta-based National Data Corporation, to speed up the reporting and consolidation of the deposits from their vast banking network across the United States.

Several bankers, including the three of us from the postal services committee, who represented the more aggressive institutions in cash management, were selected to serve on a similar committee for the United States Government General Services Administration. The purpose for the committee was to study ways to improve their cash management systems.

There were a dozen bankers included in this group. However, it was unwieldy and the GSA was slow to implement change. After a few meetings I concluded my participation was not critical and resigned. Overall, my experience with the cash management project at First National, for the two-year period, was highly rewarding and instructive. The education and experience significantly advanced my knowledge of the banking industry.

Being less sensitive to the political issues in the company and my willingness to assume the responsibility in the development of this program, when no one else would take the risk and volunteer for the job, presented a great opportunity. Frankly, because of my low status in the bank there was really not much for me to lose.

As the old proverb runs: "When you slide down the banister of life don't get a splinter in your career." But, splinters do make life more stimulating and exciting, if you can handle the pain.

Chapter Four
Too Stupid To Quit

During those years it seemed as if management change was a way of life. We experienced a number of major reorganizations at First National during my seven years of employment.

Most of the key executives were very talented people, but unfortunately some of them had a difficult time working together as a team. This is certainly not uncommon in many organizations where driven egos and career advancement prevent personal chemistry from working, as it should.

Musical Chairs among the executives in many organizations seemed to be a common occurrence. As time passed, most senior managers, at least those who survived appeared to enjoy the confusion and opportunity for advancement made available by the frequent and quixotic turnover of corporate executives.

First National, as did most of the Atlanta banks, continued to prosper and grow rapidly, while the city grew physically in all directions from the immigration of people and relocation from out- of-state companies.

The population of the Atlanta region was about 1.3 million when my family came to the city in early 1968. Today, 2003, the Atlanta SMSA, consisting of 18 counties, is now over four million people.

During the later years at First National, it became apparent that my future opportunity for advancement was limited at the bank for several significant reasons.

First, I was not a commercial lender and had not obtained any lending experience during my employment at the bank. As a general rule, most senior managers are typically trained and promoted from the credit management side of the bank, because that function provides the most profitability and stature.

Second, I was not born or raised in Atlanta and was not a member of any significant local family.

Both of these issues were important career considerations in my mind.

Deciding to undertake a master's degree program in business, I reasoned enhanced academic credentials might provide a better opportunity to advance to a more senior position.

I applied to Georgia State University in downtown Atlanta. Unfortunately, my Graduate Record Examination, which had been administered in Vietnam, was not high enough to meet the admission standards of the school's excellent business program.

My case was pleaded with the Dean of the Business School. Recalling for him my past military record, age, and recent business success I believed should count for something in their admission decision. Furthermore, it just seemed ridiculous to "simple-minded" me that they would demand a retest. Surely my qualifications were adequate. Also, after being out of college for over 9 years and not accustomed to taking academic examinations, should have some bearing in their evaluation. These were critical points in my thinking.

The Dean seemed to be impressed with my passion and offered to provide special counseling to assist in the reexamination. But, he made it perfectly clear that it would be absolutely necessary for me to score higher on the GRE in order to qualify for the College of Business at Georgia State.

Frustrated, disappointed and angry, I declined his offer for assistance and decided to do without the degree and somehow develop a successful track record on my own. The only option was to "muscle" it through with hard work and commitment. This was the course laboriously pursued throughout the remainder of my business career. Needless to say, it was a long, painful learning experience.

Without question I would have been better prepared for a business career with the advanced degree, but hard work eventually pays off, if you are dedicated, mentally committed, and willing to make the necessary personal sacrifices to achieve your objective. **"Or if one is just too stupid to quit."** My strongest personal trait, as described by my "close personal friends."

Nepotism prevailed in some banking organizations, but finally gave way when it became obvious, during some difficult years in the financial services industry that qualified human talent was more important in maintaining profitability than bloodlines.

First National had a reputation as the "Blue-Blood Bank" of Atlanta when I first joined the company. But, it probably inured to their benefit in the acquisition of business, because family members and friends would normally direct some of their wealth to those institutions. A few of the other larger banks in the city had somewhat similar reputations.

Destiny continued to play a major role in my life through my acquaintances and business associates.

Upon joining the bank, Patrick (Pat) Thomas, who was also working in the operations division selling automated payroll services, became a good friend.

Pat had been a Captain in the U. S. Army and had joined the company about six months before me. With our military backgrounds, interest in the physical side of life, and competitive natures we found we had much in common, and our personalities immediately jelled upon meeting.

Pat encouraged me to join the downtown YMCA and we subsequently spent many hours together on the small, indoor 36 laps-to-the-mile circular track, running like madmen, while trying to stay in good physical condition.

To say we were obsessive with our training habits would be a blatant understatement. We were driven overachievers, probably in everything we attempted throughout our careers.

The "Y" was a wonderful hangout and provided an opportunity to meet a vast number of professional people, who had similar goals of physical fitness in their character makeup.

The downtown facility was located on Luckie Street, just a few blocks from the bank. Its central location to the primary business center of Atlanta helped draw members from all walks of life.

It was a veritable melting pot of people, talents, jobs, and race. Our membership included attorneys, judges, bankers, real estate developers, bus drivers, salesmen, laborers, physicians, politicians, and former professional athletes.

When we arrived and put on our grungy workout gear, everyone assumed the common denominator of a "jock," and the resultant camaraderie among the members was outstanding.

My daily attendance and blind dedication to an aggressive conditioning program would eventually open the door for me with my next job at First Georgia Bank. This occurred because of my acquaintance with the bank's Chairman and former Governor of Georgia, Carl E. Sanders, who also worked out regularly at the "Y."

Carl had been an athlete at the University of Georgia and he kept himself in excellent physical condition. Apparently, he appreciated seeing this same trait in other people.

He was the principal and managing partner of a large law firm in Atlanta, Troutman, Sanders, Lockerman, and Ashmore. It was located in the old Candler Building on Peachtree Street, which also housed the main office of a small financial institution, Peoples American Bank. In time it would eventually become First Georgia Bank, after several mergers and a name change.

During these very early years in our banking careers neither Pat nor I realized what the future held in store for us. He was a damned good and successful salesman peddling banking services for FNB in the Atlanta market, while I was probably the oldest trainee, at age 31, in the history of the bank.

Simply stated, we were working hard, but maybe not smart, trying to make a name and an establish a reputation at First National, with no perception or idea of what our ultimate goals should be.

Destiny would occupy an important position in this early relationship, causing our futures to intersect frequently over the next 27 years in almost everything we undertook professionally.

Ultimately, Pat would join First Georgia about three years prior to me and start a data processing company, First Financial Management Corporation Inc., (FFMC).

Initially, the company was a part of the Georgia Railroad Bank of Augusta and was formed to provide computer accounting services to the smaller banks in Georgia.

Later, FFMC purchased The Georgia Railroad Bank's data processing department for about $1 million, further increasing its customer base and ties with the parent.

"The Georgia" was also referred to as "The Railroad Bank," because it actually owned a railroad line in Georgia.

At the conclusion of the Civil War, the company provided free transportation for many of the Southern veterans returning home.

The history of Georgia Railroad organization started in 1835 when it began banking operations in Georgia after obtaining an amendment to its charter. This change allowed the company to raise funds to build a railroad in the state.

In 1836, plans were finalized to link the Georgia Railroad line from Augusta with a rail line out of Macon, Georgia, and the Western and Atlantic railroad running south from the Tennessee State line.

Legislation was passed to obtain the necessary funding and the Georgia railroad management selected a spot on the map of Georgia where the lines would converge.

The location was called Terminus (meaning the end of a transportation line). It had at one time been the site of a Cherokee settlement, and then later a home for a tavern called White Hall.

By 1840, people began to settle around the tavern and the community then became known as Marthasville, named in honor of the Governor's daughter.

In 1845, the Georgia Railroad line reached this tiny settlement of 500 people. The Macon line arrived in 1846, and in 1847 the small community's name was changed to Atlanta.

In 1851, the northern line from Tennessee finally linked-up with the other two railway lines.

Interestingly, the name for this inauspicious community was selected by the chief engineer of the Georgia Railroad and Banking Company, who had directed the construction of the rail line from Augusta to Atlanta.

Many years later, people associated with the Augusta bank believed "The Georgia," through its ownership of the railroad, was primarily responsible for the creation of Atlanta.

There always seems to be some "minor" enviousness in existence between the smaller towns and the large cities in every state. It is called hometown pride.

"The Railroad Bank" owned 5% of First Georgia, from an earlier investment promoted by their former chairman, Sherman Drawdy. He envisioned this investment as a way for the Augusta bank to eventually acquire a location in Atlanta when the State branching laws were changed.

This was the maximum ownership of a bank allowed by another financial institution in the state of Georgia. It would be several years before that regulation was changed allowing Georgia financial institutions to open branches statewide, acquire banks in Georgia or in contiguous states, and start-up de novo operations.

The Georgia Railroad Bank formed a new holding company in the late seventies and adopted the name First Railroad and Banking Company of Georgia. Its principal subsidiary, the Augusta based bank, would still be referred to as the "Georgia," and the railroad line, consisting of nothing more than tracks, would be finally sold in the early eighties.

In 1982, First Financial tendered and purchased most of the stock of their company, which was then owned by several smaller stockholder banks and First Railroad. It was finally spun-off as a publicly held company, trading first on the NASDAQ and later on the New York Stock Exchange. First Railroad eventually sold their ownership position some time later.

FFMC would ultimately be greatly successful, primarily through Pat's initiative, as it migrated into one of the largest Information Services Companies in the country with several operating subsidiaries and $4 billion in revenues.

First Data Corporation eventually purchased FFMC in October 1995 for over $7 billion in stock. Not a bad return on investment when considering the original capitalization was only $600,000 and debt of about $1 million.

First Georgia Bank had provided $200,000 of those funds as an initial stockholder and would sell its one-third interest back to First Railroad, at their insistence, before FFMC went public.

Looking back on that transaction, it can easily be determined by any amateur that this was not a favorable transaction to First Georgia. If the bank could have retained its ownership, the initial investment would have grown in value to one billion dollars eventually.

Pat provided the brains and supplied the vision for FFMC. He surprised many skeptical people with the ultimate success of the company. It would become a Fortune 500 company before it was sold.

I would eventually complete my business career working for Pat, starting at the time FFMC bought Georgia Federal from Fuqua Industries in 1989.

Three years later, when the bank was sold to First Union Corporation in Charlotte, I was appointed as the chief operations officer of FFMC and finally a vice-chairman, and occupied that position until my retirement two months prior to the purchase by First Data Corporation in 1995.

As previously noted, destiny seemingly has an all-encompassing way of impacting people's lives in the most unusual, far-reaching, and convoluted manner.

If Pat and I had not become friends early on and possessed some of the same mental characteristics and backgrounds to build a friendship, who knows what might have eventually occurred during my business life?

We started our careers at about the same time, while working together at First National, and later as subsidiary presidents of different companies, both owned and controlled by First Railroad.

The similarities of our backgrounds, paralleling careers, and the ultimate conclusion of our business lives, almost simultaneously, must have received some orchestration by someone or something outside of normal reasoning. It was just too coincidental to have evolved by chance.

Our old melting pot, the downtown "Y" was finally closed, and the building razed in the early eighties. The membership had declined, because many companies relocated to the outskirts of the city taking with them a large portion of the membership.

At the closing ceremony, which was attended by many of the last existing members, Carl Sanders was recognized for his efforts to keep the facility operating during the decline. He had raised considerable funds during the previous years to help maintain and support the "Y." He also had the longest tenure of any current member.

A piece of memorabilia for my 20-year membership and efforts to also help maintain the facility during those faltering years was given to me at the ceremony.

It was my metal locker basket, which had been used to store my jock gear. It had been freshly painted, covering the rust from my sweaty workout clothes. It had a small gold plaque attached with my name and years of membership inscribed. I had probably sweated enough through those 20-odd years of workouts to fill that basket several times. The container is still in my possession and I frequently recall the fond memories and friends of those years.

In the mid-seventies many of the members, who liked to jog at noon, made a major transition in their running program and left the old indoor track and started jogging in the streets of downtown Atlanta, over to the central city Piedmont Park, and around the downtown Georgia Tech campus.

It was in 1974 when the outdoor running craze really began in this city and the Peachtree Road race took on significance, as more people popularized this running event by joining the yearly increasing number of contestants. The participants in 2003 were in excess of 55,000.

The noontime run from the "Y" was a daily occurrence for many of us and further cemented the friendships of the members as we joined together in small groups to "beat the cement" in our rudimentary Adidas or Nike running shoes.

When driving downtown on those old running paths of concrete, my memories at the "Y" are pleasantly reinforced, as I recall those enjoyable and stress releasing jaunts through the streets of Atlanta from the late sixties to the mid-nineties.

Destiny walked into my office in the early summer of 1974 in the person of the Executive Vice President of First Georgia Bank, Cliff Hornsby. He had previously worked at First National for several years and had joined First Georgia Bank in 1970.

After some conversation he informed me he would be leaving the company in a few weeks, for undisclosed reasons, and believed I should seek the position he was vacating.

He knew that I was looking for a better opportunity to advance my career and he said to me, "this is it."

I had been mulling over my future at First National for some time and had concluded that an opportunity for an executive senior management position would not be presented in the near future.

Approaching 38 years of age, after almost seven years with First National, it was time to either make the commitment to see it through at the bank and hope for the best, or go to more fertile territory, if I could find it.

As the result of the conversation with Hornsby, I decided to apply for the job at First Georgia and to speak with the Chairman, Carl Sanders.

As I had made his acquaintance at the YMCA he recognized my name on the inquiry and agreed to talk with me about the position.

Carl was gracious and seemingly interested during our discussion, but when he was told of my background, which was primarily operational in nature, with no lending experience, his light and interest seemed to dim. I knew immediately a credible and convincing point had to be made quickly or the game would be over.

I was selling, begging, and pleading in anticipation he would, at least, give me some small amount of consideration during the job search.

When talking with Carl, during the interview, he convinced me the job was a great opportunity without actually offering me the position. He told me that no manager would ever have as much freedom, authority, or fun in a large institution as I could have running a smaller bank like First Georgia. He was baiting me and it worked.

Being most persistent, following up with phone messages and written correspondence for the next several weeks, probably making a major nuisance of myself, I vowed not to quit in this pursuit until a final decision of some kind was made.

In the Marine Corps we were taught to never quit until you completed your mission or achieved your objective. In my mind I definitely had a mission and an objective.

My persistence or obsession with matters like this is best explained by a comment and observation made to me by a Navy doctor, who was the surgeon of our battalion in Vietnam.

One evening on a typical monsoon rainy night we were having a libation and some general conversation about our future after the war, while sitting in our tent in Dong Ha, South Vietnam, just a few miles below the Demilitarized Zone. I told him, during our discussion, about a recent decision to resign my commission from the Corps, when my tour of duty was completed. My goal would then be to make a "living" in the civilian business world.

After a couple more shooters of liquor, while we were leisurely sitting on our bunk rolls, I asked him if he thought I could be successful in business. He had another sip of his drink, deliberated for a moment and then he said; "Yes, I think you will be very successful."

After a few minutes and another drink, filled with inquisitiveness, I had to ask why he was so confident of my ability to succeed with a change in careers. He looked straight at me and without blinking an eye or displaying a smile, in total seriousness, he responded: **"Because you're too damned stupid to know when to quit."**

That was it. He captured the essence of my character with his statement. It probably does, fortunately or unfortunately, describe my strongest personal trait, and illustrates perfectly the reason I would not stop pestering Carl Sanders in my pursuit of the First Georgia opportunity.

This is not all bad. It definitely helps maintain focus and an unrelenting dedication toward finishing the job. How many times has someone failed simply because they lost the initiative momentarily, and gave in when they should have stayed the course? To be successful in this world I think it is very important to never quit, particularly if you have the power of your convictions firmly established in your personal mindset.

The devotion to this mentality and persistence has unquestionably been repeated many times throughout my life. After suffering through many errors of judgement, inappropriate decisions, and embarrassing situations this characteristic has probably saved my ass, reputation, and job more times than anyone would care to admit---including me.

After meeting with Carl, nothing happened for a couple of weeks. My family and I headed to the beach for a vacation.

After a couple of days, the desire for the job was burning in my stomach. I called several times to see how the search was going. Obviously making a continuing nuisance of myself.

Carl finally acquiesced and asked me to join him in Augusta where he would be attending a bank board meeting. He wanted a few of the senior management members of the Georgia Railroad Bank to meet me, as they were part owners of First Georgia.

When you want something badly enough or you have a mission, never take anything for granted. Always assume there is one more thing that needs to be done.

So I called Pat Thomas, who had now been with that organization for three years and was managing FFMC, and asked him to put in a good word for me. He had already spoken to Carl earlier and told me he would speak to him again. With that done, I drove from the beach in South Carolina to meet my new destiny.

Following a short discussion with Sanders, he then introduced me to Charles Presley, the Chairman of the bank and Quincy McPherson, who was the President and a former executive with the First National Bank of Atlanta in his previous life.

After some pleasantries, we talked about the position and they questioned me extensively for about an hour. The meeting and interview ended abruptly and the three of them huddled together for a few minutes. They concluded and informed me, without any formality, that the job was mine.

Carl had already made the decision, and we were only going through the process with the other executives to give them the opportunity to participate in the final decision.

We concluded our discussions with my acceptance, and I drove five hours back to the beach to meet my family with the good news.

Some weeks later, after joining the bank, it would become apparent the news was not really that good. There were many problems festering within the bowels of the bank. They had not yet surfaced, but they were ready for exploitation, and only a slight nudge was needed for them to spring forth. I was not the only one who was unaware of the situation.

The bank was going south quickly, because of some serious problems in the loan portfolio. No one had the faintest idea of just how bad the issues were, including the senior management, who wouldn't admit it if they did. The uniformed board of directors, and the Executives in Augusta at the Georgia Railroad Bank were also very much in the dark.

Unfortunately, First Georgia Bank was a disaster looking for a place to happen and it was going to happen on my watch.

It appeared I was going back into combat, but this time no one was shooting real bullets. However, the likelihood for survival in this business situation was just unlikely as being trapped in the killing zone of a Vietcong ambush in the Vietnam jungles. There would be casualties in both cases.

Upon returning from my vacation and immediately tendering my resignation to Ben Rawlins at First National the decision was now cast in concrete. Ben understood my position and wished me good luck. He was both my boss and an understanding friend.

The resignation letter was forwarded on to Raymond Riddle, the President of the bank, whom I respected and admired very much. He was also a good friend and appreciated the work that had been done in the past to support his previous organization.

To his credit, he made a noble effort trying to persuade me to stay with First National. Aware of my concern for future advancement, he offered to provide some personalized credit training, which would improve my status in the bank, and then transfer me into a corporate lending division as soon as possible.

He indicated this would enhance my banking career and likelihood of promotion. Raymond was a professional and quality executive in every respect.

It was too little too late. My decision had been made and it was time to get on with the next phase of my life. However, this new career opportunity would be on shaky ground for more years than could be fathomed at the time.

Fortunately, I was not business savvy enough to recognize the seriousness of the problems with my new company and how they could affect my career if the bank failed.

Now, thinking back about those times, with a great deal more maturity and experience, and considering my propensity to tackle issues with reckless abandonment, it is likely I would have still taken the job.

The challenge to take on something adventurous and challenging, like the First Georgia Bank situation would still be too great an opportunity to decline.

At times, when faced with an uncertain decision or situation where the outcome is questionable and your critics are overwhelmingly negative, it may be helpful to recall the Bumblebee analogy.

Aerodynamics refutes the Bumblebee's ability to fly, because his small wings are not large enough for his oversized body. But, the bumblebee doesn't know anything about aerodynamics so he just goes ahead and flies.

I reported to First Georgia Bank in late August 1974 to assume the responsibilities and title as the Executive Vice President and Chief Operating Officer of the bank.

If it had not been for Carl Sanders this opportunity to advance my career in banking would not have occurred. He had spent a great deal of time deliberating on my capabilities during the interview process, or so it seemed to me at the time, when in reality he had made up his mind early and was testing me to determine how strongly I wanted the job.

After joining the bank, and eventually achieving a successful track record, Carl would tell people the reason he hired me was because of my tenacity.

He would explain; "I saw this seemingly determined young man running around the track at the YMCA day after day. After our bank got into trouble and discovered he was a banker, I thought he was the kind of person we needed to turn our problem company around."

Carl always followed through on what he told you. No one can ask for more than that from his or her mentor. He has remained a good friend over the years, and I will always revere his support and guidance from those difficult early years at First Georgia Bank.

There is a Marine Corps axiom that has been a standard practice and belief of that "tight fisted" organization for many years. It was appropriate for what was about to be endured at First Georgia Bank. "We have done so much so long with so little, soon we will be able to do everything with nothing."

**First National Bank of Atlanta officer and Marine veteran
Awarded Silver Star at Marine Headquarters in Atlanta, 1968.
Official U. S. Marine Corps Photo.**

**First National Bank of Atlanta Cash Management Team, 1972.
Robert Pledger, Mike Petway, Trica Hand and Tildon Smith.
Provided by author.**

First Georgia Bank Management Team, 1975.
Leland E. Petit, Ralph W. King, Joe K. Steele, John L. Johnson
Robert A. Calvert, Author, Malcom C. Garland, Tony K. Miller
Provided by Author.

Author signs Honest Face Agreement with
Tom Williams, Chairman, First National Bank, 1977.
Atlanta Business Chronicle.

First Georgia Bank's Women's Banking Committee.
Mary Lewis Preston; Jean F. Caldwell; Ann P. Henshaw;
Andrea S. James; Lorraine Clark; Peggy B. Hull, 1977.
Provided by Author.

Charles Presley, Chairman First Railroad and Banking
Company of Georgia and Author, 1978.

Atlanta Business Chronicle.

Author and Carl E. Sanders, Chairman, 1981.
Conway Atlanta Photography.

"First Georgia Bank is as progressive as Atlanta."
MARVIN ARRINGTON, ATTORNEY, ARRINGTON, RUBIN, WINTER & GOGER, P.C.

With Marvin Arrington, right, are Carl Sanders, Jr., First Georgia director Tom Cordy, Peggy Hull and Mal Garland of First Georgia.

"First Georgia understands the unique problems of women in the business world."
FLORENCE CLOUDT, PRESIDENT, FOCAL POINT INC.

Florence Cloudt is with First Georgia director Deen Day and banker Ann Henshaw.

"First Georgia fits our growing needs."
JACK BRADY, PRESIDENT, ANDERSEN 2000 INC.

Jack Brady, right, is shown with Mike Marshall, Andersen 2000 Inc., and Don Kimbel of First Georgia.

First Georgia Bank Financial Highlights, 1982.
Provided by Author

Author, Don Ratajczak, Georgia State University; Joe Torre, Manager, Atlanta Braves at customer breakfast, 1982.
Conway Atlanta Photography

Mary Lou Austin, Executive Director, Atlanta USO; Author; Maria Osmond; unidentified Marine; Mrs. Osmond; Washington D. C. USO meeting, 1983.
Provided by Author.

**First Georgia Bank Management Team at Christmas party, 1983.
Ralph King; Richard Hunt; Don Stahle; Jim Box; Jim Spies;
Terry Miller, and Author.
Provided by Author.**

**Author "ragged out" on Outward Bound, 1984.
Provided by Author.**

Brown   Guyton

Jackson   Jones

Strickland   Williams

The Banking Leaders of Atlanta in the eighties.
Bennett Brown, C&S National; Robert Guyton, National Bank of
Georgia; Author, First Georgia; Gordon Jones, Fulton National;
Robert Strickland, Sun Trust; Thomas Williams, First National.
Atlanta Business Chronicle.

**Tom Peters, author of In Search of Excellence, with First Georgia
executives, Terry Miller; Judy Horton; and Richard Hunt, 1984.
First Georgia Bank Highlights.**

**First Georgia Bank management team, top to bottom, left to right.
Don Stahle; Richard Hunt; Ed Milligan; Judy Horton; Terry Miller;
Grady Coleman; James Spies; Ralph King; James Box, 1986.
First Georgia Bank Highlights.**

**Author and new CEO of Georgia Federal Bank standing beside
Chairman John B. Zellars, July 1986.
Atlanta Journal-Constitution.**

**Author, "pressing the flesh" with Bernie Marcus,
Chairman Home Depot Inc., 1987.
Conway Atlanta, Photography.**

**Chairman J. B. Fuqua, foreground, and President Lawrence Klamon
Fuqua Industries, Inc., 1987.
Atlanta Journal-Constitution.**

**Author with a few of the managers at Georgia Federal, 1988.
Provided by Author.**

**Executives of First Financial Management, Inc., 1989
E. Douglas Schachner, Chief Financial Officer; M. Tarlton Pittard, Senior
Executive Vice President; Patrick Thomas, Chairman and CEO; Author.
Georgia Federal Bank Newspaper.**

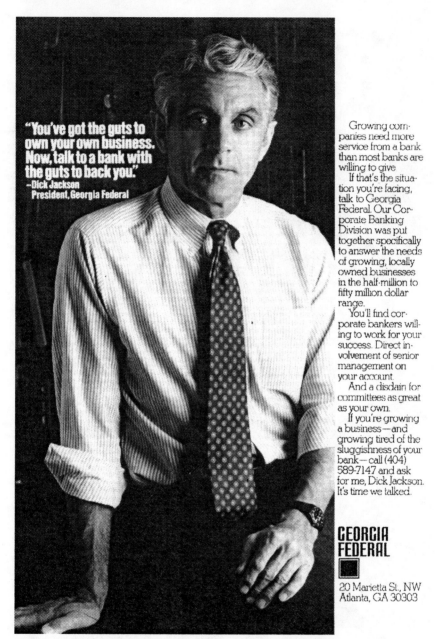

Georgia Federal Bank Newspaper Advertisement, 1990.
Provided by Author

Georgia Federal Bank Corporate Challenge run, 1991.
Georgia Federal Bank Newspaper.

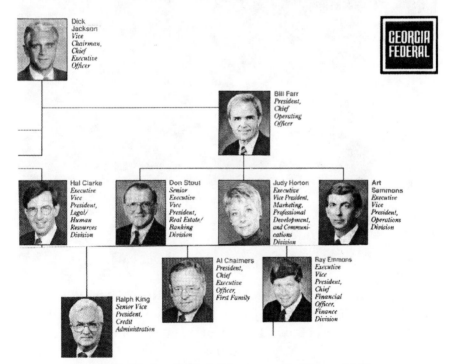

Georgia Federal Bank Management Team, 1993.
Georgia Federal Bank Newspaper.

**The sweet smell of the outdoors, Green River, Utah, 1994.
Mack Butler, former attorney with Troutman, Sanders, Lockerman
& Ashmore. James Box, CEO, eBank Financial Services Inc., and
Author.
Provided by Author.**

First Financial Management at the end of the hunt, 1995.
Pat Thomas, Chairman and CEO; Vice Chairman, Stephen D. Kane;
ViceChairman M. Tarlton Pittard; Senior Executive Vice President,
Randolph L Hutto; Director, George Cohen;
Vice Chairman Robert J. Amnan and Author.
Provided by Author.

tlanta's top
ommercial
eal estate brokers

ndustry Focus
Commercial
eal Estate
ection C

ATLANTA BUSINESS CHRONICLE

Commanding presence: Former high-ranking military commanders now in business in Atlanta include, from left, Marine Major Richard Jackson, Army Lt. Gen. Dan Benton and Navy Vice Adm. Scott Redd.

BYRON E. SMALL

From battlefield to business

By Lisa R. Schoolcraft
STAFF WRITER

As U.S. military commanders lead coalition troops in Iraq, other former high-ranking commanders are leading Atlanta companies, law firms and educational organizations.

Dan Benton, director of European development for shoe retailer **Athlete's Foot Group**, is a retired U.S. Army lieutenant general. Bob Bunker, CEO of electronics firm **TGA Technologies Inc.**, is a retired Army major general. Ed Burba Jr., a board member or Atlanta-based **Global Payments Inc.**, is a retired

Former Marine Corps Major Jackson spent eight years in the service, first in Cuba during the Cuban Missile Crisis in 1962, and later, as commander of a rifle company in Vietnam. Afterward, he served as president of First Georgia Bank and Georgia Federal Savings Bank.

Jackson says his military service taught him the value of training.

"Before I went to Vietnam, I learned how to locate and defuse booby traps, which was a weapon highly used in Vietnam," he said. Once while on patrol in Vietnam, he heard a light click and realized he had stepped on the trip wire of a booby trap. He pushed his radio operator,

yelled "Run!" and got 10 feet before the booby trap exploded, he said.

"If I had not put myself through this training and learned how to deal with it, I'd be dead today," Jackson said. "There is never enough training."

That carries over into customer service and sales training in any business, too. "[Employees] have got to be prepared for whatever may come," he said.

April 4-10, 2003

Atlanta Business Chronicle, 2003.

Chapter Five
First Georgia Bank

First Georgia Bank, with $100 million in deposits, was the sixth largest financial institution in Atlanta in 1974 and the twenty-second largest bank in the state. Citizens and Southern was the largest bank in Georgia, followed by First National, Trust Company, Fulton National, and the National Bank of Georgia.

There were a number of smaller banks scattered throughout the Atlanta community and several Savings and Loan institutions, including Decatur Federal, Fulton Federal and Georgia Federal. All of these institutions were much larger in assets and deposits than First Georgia.

First Georgia Bancshares Holding Company was the principal owner of the bank and Georgia Railroad and Banking Company of Augusta owned 5%, as a result of an earlier investment in 1972, which was then allowed by state law.

In 1973, First Georgia Bancshares, a public company, borrowed eight million dollars from a large bank in New York City and purchased the Bank of Fulton County in East Point, Georgia. Prior to that acquisition, Bancshares had previously acquired both the Peoples and American Banks in Atlanta, and the resultant three merged banks became First Georgia Bank.

Bancshares intended to do another public offering later that year and repay the debt from their New York lender. By the end of 1973 the stock market weakened and Bancshares decided to wait until conditions improved. They didn't. Economic conditions worsened significantly throughout the year. Starting in 1974, the faltering economy and the rise of the prime rate to its highest point in modern history, along with the souring real estate loans caused most bank earnings to drop acutely.

First Georgia was unable to pay the quarterly interest payment on the new debt in September just as I came on board. The note matured in December of that year and the debt had blossomed to over $9 million with the accrued unpaid interest.

All indicators, for both the current and future prospects of the company, were headed down and getting worse as the economy continued to deteriorate almost daily.

By November, loans were being charged off for either non-payment or bankruptcy at a rapid pace. These same loan problems would continue to create difficult financial problems for First Georgia and the other Atlanta banks throughout 1975.

The Atlanta business climate would suffer as one of the worst in the country, because of the heavy investment directed toward real estate development during the prior years.

The city in the sixties and early seventies was primarily a real estate oriented community, but has since blossomed into a multi-faceted business economy. Much of the impetus to this diversification occurred as a result of the previous climate and the terrible financial conditions preceding the business decline.

First Georgia Bank lost several million dollars in 1974, primarily from loan charge-offs and non-performing loans. By the end of that year the bank's assets had declined by over $30 million to $75 million. Total assets had topped $110 million prior to its fall from grace. It was now approaching insolvency with unacceptable capital levels to support the balance sheet and meet regulatory requirements.

In addition, the cost structure of the bank was completely out of control. Prior management had no idea how to stop the downhill slide of the company or position it to regain profitability in the slumping market.

Fortunately, after considerable soul searching, the board of directors, chaired by Carl Sanders, realized the dire conditions. A restructuring plan, promoted by the Atlanta Federal Reserve Bank, and supported by the State Banking Department, with the cooperation of the Georgia Railroad Bank, was agreed upon by the directors and hastily implemented.

Under the proposed plan the loan now held by Chemical Bank in New York would be guaranteed by the Georgia Railroad Bank, much to their chagrin, but was an absolute requirement of the lenders.

In addition, the Railroad Bank would purchase three million dollars of preferred stock in First Georgia to support the devastated capital position of the bank. This was to be converted into an 80% ownership of the company at some future date when the banking laws permitted.

The Georgia Railroad Bank agreed to belly up to the bar, so to speak, and take a large financial risk, but in the long run it worked out to be a great business investment for them.

Losses in the loan portfolio continued to mount at First Georgia before the deal was completed and the new capital was injected. Classified loans represented 185% of capital. Normally, 20% would have been considered excessive and caused regulatory intervention.

This large percentage of adverse loans was reason enough for the Federal Reserve to close or sell the bank if a buyer would have shown any interest, which none did.

Economic conditions were continuing to deteriorate around the country and many economists were predicting a depression.

About this time I heard a comedian one evening on television describe the difference between a recession and a depression. He said, "a recession occurs when people who can't afford to pay quit buying, and a depression begins when people who never intended to pay in the first place quit buying."

First Georgia must have had a lot of people from that latter group as their customers, because a large percentage quit paying on their loans during that time. Thankfully, the economy did not ultimately sink into a depression.

Many banks around the country were experiencing similar loan problems due to the sick economy. The purchase of a troubled bank in a problem market was not very appealing to any acquiring-minded institution. There were few "White Knights" willing to do battle for an acquisition, or invest their money in a questionable deal, under these circumstances.

The only available options for the bank were to close the doors or go with the capital deal structure with The Railroad Bank, which was only minimally acceptable to the regulatory agencies.

As a result of the efforts and support of Monroe Kimball, the President of the Atlanta Fed, and a friend of many of the principals involved, the proposal was accepted, and new life was temporarily breathed into the uncertain future of First Georgia Bank.

Now, even though the company had weathered the storm, there were no guarantees the bank could earn a profit in 1975, or for that matter, ever achieve a future profitable level of operations.

Later, after Mr. Kimball retired from the Atlanta Federal Reserve Bank, he accepted a position as the Vice-Chairman of First Railroad and Banking Company of Georgia, formerly the Georgia Railroad Bank of Augusta. He remained in that role for several years.

He brought a great deal of expertise and stature to the organization and helped build First Railroad in size and prominence during his tenure in that position.

It was under these circumstances I started my new job at First Georgia in 1974, and was made President and CEO of the bank a few months later.

The current President, Cotty Graves, was also a First National Bank graduate. He had been brought into the company by Andy Huber, whom he had worked for at his former bank.

Cotty, a very nice man, but with little bank management operating experience, resigned due to the financial problems surrounding the company, all of which occurred on his watch. His resignation prompted my rapid elevation to his vacated position.

Some of my friends, who were aware of the troubles at the bank, said my promotion had similarities to Custer's last stand at the Little Bighorn River. They told me, "you just happened to be the last white man standing after the Indian attack."

At our board meeting, one of the bank's directors, Carl Sutherland, a former General in the Army and director of personnel for the city of Atlanta, summed up my appointment under the dire conditions of the company rather pointedly. He said to the other members of the directorate, "It is a hollow honor at best."

Trying to be philosophical about the whole matter I told some my associates; "It's better to be in charge of something than nothing." My lack of business acumen prevented me from realizing just how impossible the situation was.

Fortunately, the bank had some dedicated bankers in a few key positions. That was a positive. The negative was that none of the managers had a clue about the serious issues facing First Georgia or understood how the bank had gotten into such a terrible financial condition. It appeared prior senior management, even if they actually realized how serious the bank's financial condition was, had kept many of the issues hidden from both the employees and directors.

It didn't take long to discover what was going on in the company. Chuck Ford, the chief financial officer, had attempted to bring understanding to the previous executive management, but had gotten no support in resolving any of the problems.

Spurred by his expertise, knowledge, and able assistance, we were able to at least begin to understand the issues, and started developing a plan of attack.

The first action taken was to identify and place the non-performing loans on non-accrual and charge off those that were worthless. The prior management team had failed to address these issues totally. They had continued to accrue interest on these assets and report income, even when the customers were unable to make any payments.

The bank then ceased to show a profit and went into the "red" with losses in excess of $250 thousand per month for the remainder of the year.

There were no controls in place to monitor the bank's activities and no formal budgetary process.

The entire operation had been run by the seat of the pants of the former executive staff. Most of those managers had by now left the bank or would soon be departing with executive and board encouragement.

Communications to the staff from management had ceased, and the mushroom effect, i.e., keeping everyone in the dark, seemed to be practiced routinely.

There was no business plan, no strategy, no goals or objectives, and no measurement tools of any kind to be found within the confines of the company.

First Georgia's assets were also shrinking equally from the result of bad publicity. Customers were closing their accounts and leaving the institution as a result of the negative press that was beginning to appear in the newspaper.

Loans were deteriorating by the day and no one in the lending area had any real grasp of what was happening to the portfolio or how to stop the bleeding.

The organization had been run like a country club with full access given to anyone who wanted a sweetheart deal.

Confusion and poor morale were rampant and there was no evidence of leadership to be found in any crevice within the bank.

Those who tried to identify and correct the problems were either summarily dismissed by the bank executive team or beaten down to protect the offenders.

Finally, there was no process in place to control the bank's expenses, and in fact, management did not have any idea how or where they were spending money.

This was a case of good intentions gone bad, which was caused by inexperience, a lack of knowledge of what to do about the problems, reluctance to initiate any actions, and fear to honestly face-up to the issues. Management had opted not to report the situation as it existed and hope the situation would somehow resolve itself.

In short, the bank was out-of-control and in one hell of a mess. Even I could make that assessment with my limited experience.

Pogo, the cartoon character, described the bank's management attitude perfectly in one of famous comedy comments to his friends when he said: "There is no problem so big that it cannot be run away from."

There is a theme about history saying it often repeats itself. "Therein lies the rub," as Shakespeare composed in Hamlet's Soliloquy.

The situation with the bank, at that time, was similar to an assignment given to me in Vietnam in 1966.

I was put in charge of a rifle company that was in disarray and nearly ineffective as a fighting combat unit. The company had been beaten-up rather badly by the enemy, morale was low, the current commander was "tired," and the company's performance was deteriorating by the day.

The major difference, of course, was that no one was shooting real bullets at the bank.

My mission, in no uncertain terms, as expressed by my battalion commander in a very brief, but concise conversation, was to "get my young ass out to the company position and get the fucking mess squared away, and be prepared to move out in the attack. And do it ASAP."

Those were precise instructions and they didn't leave any room for questions. However, the devil is always in the details.

Of course, first Georgia was not in a war and Atlanta was not Vietnam, but the same kind of commitment, teamwork, and leadership was required to resolve the situation at both the bank and the rifle company. Any organization, whether in combat or business, requires the same kind of diligence and "guts" to get the job done, if it is going to survive and win.

A tenet of war fighting taught in the Corps provided the best guidance for our action plan. "When in doubt attack. Keep attacking and trying different stuff and until you find something that works, but most importantly never quit trying."

This was to become our hallmark for action. The plan was clear. We would not hesitate to move quickly and decisively. We would attack the problems, using all available resources, and move forward aggressively. There were no other options.

Extensive efforts were implemented to improve the morale of the bank's "troops" by recognizing their accomplishments and providing constant communication to ensure they understood the objectives and strategy.

Our costs were so far out of line we had to reduce staff and close down some of our operations. We moved all of our operating facilities into the small basement of the Candler Building, where our main banking office and headquarters were located to reduce our rental expenses.

We approached our outside vendors and asked for moratoriums on service contracts. Not only could we not afford to pay them on a normal basis going forward, but we also needed the current bills reduced in order to stay viable for the present.

Our Accountants, Peat, Marwick, & Mitchell understood the problems as well any anyone, and through the efforts of one of their partners, Neal Purcell, our senior account representative, we were able to gain a reduction in their billing structure.

We pleaded our case by telling all of our vendors; **"It was better to bend than break."** We would find a way to amicably and fairly settle the equation in the future, after we recovered from our dismal financial condition.

Our legal representation provided by Troutman, Sanders, Lockerman, and Ashmore also had to "bite the bullet" on their bills. Carl Sanders, our Chairman and senior partner of the firm, helped greatly in facilitating this arrangement.

Not only could we not afford to pay for our legal expenses, but also we had to have more attorneys assigned to help with our troubled loan portfolio of nearly $20 million.

Mack O. Butler, a senior partner of the law firm, who became a good friend and camping buddy, provided the principal representation and was assisted ably and professionally by six young, bright, and dedicated attorneys.

The legal issues were so severe and critical to the bank; it became necessary to meet weekly with our lawyers for a half-day for nearly two years to ensure we had a handle on the problems, and to properly coordinate our legal actions and recovery efforts.

We actually received payments from some of these old problem loans several years after the litigation, because of the great follow-up by our team of attorneys.

Both our accountants and lawyers did a great job helping to resolve many of the problems. Without their assistance we would not have survived. Neal Purcell was the partner of the accounting firm, Peat Marwick Mitchell, who helped with our loan and accounting problems, was instrumental in our eventual recovery.

Much of the accounting work and legal representation was done without payment from the bank until we became solvent and could afford to reinstate the service agreements in full. At that time, these organizations were properly rewarded for their diligence, support, and cooperation.

When describing this period as being difficult, it is a gross understatement of the seriousness of the situation. The real truth is the bank should have either been sold or taken over by the regulatory agencies and closed permanently.

Somehow, our desire, refusal to quit, and willingness to do whatever was necessary to correct the problems must have made a positive impact on the " Powers That Be" at the Federal Reserve Bank in Atlanta and the Georgia State Banking Department. The "Fed" even supplied a bank examiner on a full time basis for several months to help us with our loan problems. This was done at our request, and they were more than willing to help us regain financial stability in lieu of closing the bank.

Robert Kennedy, when asked about Lyndon Johnson serving as the vice president to his brother, John Kennedy, said: "I would rather have him inside the tent pissing out than on the outside pissing in."

The Federal Reserve served a noble cause in helping our bank recover from its problems, and they were also definitely inside our tent.

I personally made a trip to Washington, D.C. to talk with the head of the Federal Reserve's problem bank group. Terry Bridges, an attorney with our law firm and one of the bright lawyers assisting in our clean up, accompanied me on the trip.

We had an engaging and informative meeting, while I pleaded our case and willingness to go to any end to correct the situation. My naivete was probably obvious. But, he listened attentively as we gave him a complete status report of our actions and future plans.

I deeply believed, if given the chance, we could and would be successful. The **"bumblebee analogy"** was always present in my subconscious. I didn't realize or accept the possibility that we were not supposed to succeed. Actually, I just didn't know any better and my ignorance probably helped save our ass in the long run.

The efforts put forth by Carl Sanders to influence our case for survival was simply outstanding. His confidence and belief in the bank was overwhelmingly positive. He put his reputation and stature in the community on the line when talking to the many constituents, who held our future in their grasp.

The willingness of the Georgia Railroad Bank to provide capital materially enhanced the situation, although the injection of equity was only barely acceptable under normally prescribed rules.

All of the people involved with the bank had a major influence on the defining authorities and their decision to allow the bank to live and fight another day. Never has any group of people had to go hat in hand to so many diverse parties to seek aid and assistance in what appeared to be an impossible situation.

The Georgia Railroad Bank provided their most senior credit executive, Levings Laney, to assist us with our loan problems.

Levings was near retirement when he joined First Georgia. He brought a maturity and knowledge base to our institution that was missing in the organization. He became a good friend, a loyal supporter of the bank, and significantly enhanced our credibility with the Georgia Railroad and the regulatory agencies.

He was an invaluable resource, highly respected, and his experience was instrumental in helping to achieve a successful turn-around of the company. He spent the last three years of his career living in Atlanta working diligently for First Georgia.

Humility became a way of life during those early years with the bank, and we all learned to put our personal egos aside and work together for a common goal---survival.

Once we had gained the assurances from the regulatory authorities to remain open, we began to study the market in an attempt to develop a strategic positioning and plan that would enable the bank to compete effectively in Atlanta.

We stumbled upon a strategy, almost by accident, that would eventually provide the financial salvation for the bank and propel its growth over the next several years.

First Georgia had less than 3% of the commercial banking market share in Atlanta. Consequently, we had an opportunity to solicit business from the remaining market. Of course, not all of these accounts would be appropriate for the bank due to their size and current banking arrangements.

The obvious conclusion was simple. No other bank had as much opportunity for growth as we did in this market segment. But, we had to develop a proper strategy and solicit business from those accounts that met our capabilities.

First Georgia had eight branches in the metropolitan area, which was costly for a bank our size and a major limitation in the development of consumer business. All the larger banks had a plethora of branches in the city area, giving them a much broader access to this market.

With our critical financial condition, we would not be in a position to build new branches in the near future and would ultimately be forced to close some of the less profitable and smaller offices. This would further limit our ability to generate new consumer business.

By default, this left the business markets as the logical option on which to focus our efforts. A large branch network was not essential to the development of this segment.

Our lending limit, the amount of money we could lend to a single entity, was controlled by our capital structure. This factor dictated the size of companies we could effectively service. It was concluded, upon completion of our analysis, that we could provide banking services to those companies with revenues up to $50 million. This size defined the small to medium-size corporate market.

We decided to orient our strategy to this specific sector by becoming the first dedicated **"middle market bank"** in Atlanta. No other institution in Atlanta had played this marketing card in their deck of business strategies.

Our ultimate success in this niche proved the validity of our decision and clearly demonstrated the smaller businesses were not receiving attention from the larger financial institutions at the time.

This identical approach was again validated several years later when a number of start-up banks successfully adopted similar strategies. And it worked for them just as it had for First Georgia.

All of our advertising, business development, and energy would be directed toward this single business objective for the next five years.

We began our plan by implementing an aggressive personal sales calling program, because this was the most expedient and inexpensive tactic we could employ. This allowed us to leverage our current staff without adding any additional costs. We did not have advertising money. Our only available option was to get as many "feet out on the street" as we could to tell our story and sell our products.

All officers, including the executives, were assigned prospect call quotas each month. Most would be cold calls, without appointments, as we had no sizable customer base or prospect referral lists to work from. Business development reports were submitted after the calls to validate our progress and to build future business reference files.

We started slowly, and as our confidence grew so did the sales calls, going from only thirty initially to over 1000 monthly, after a few years into this committed sales program.

If any organization makes that many contacts and solicitations on a regular basis, they are going to sell something eventually, even if they have only a limited array of products. We did have a few competitive services and were aggressive in trying to sell them. We only had to find a receptive audience.

This sales program was not an immediate success. The number of calls monthly were limited, because our folks did not have good sales skills, and they had to overcome the bad publicity about the bank when they talked to their prospects.

Nevertheless, we just kept showing up at the prospect's door, until they finally realized we were in the game to stay and would keep coming back until they bought something. Then when they did, we were going to "smother them with attention." And we did.

We epitomized a humorous story told by the motivational speaker, Herb True, at a conference hosted by the Georgia Bankers Association. He was making a point about sales calls and he related the following tale about a salesman he had met and questioned about the number of calls he reputedly made.

The alleged salesman replied; "I made 39 calls in one day and I would have made more, but some damned fool wanted to know what I was selling." The salesman was then asked, "but did you get any orders?" The salesman replied, "Yes, three, get out, stay out, and don't come back."

We used every sales motivation scheme we could conjure up in our minds. Cash incentives for success in bringing new business into the bank. Calling quotas to measure efforts in the program, and lots of recognition for giving it the old college try. Even failures were heralded as proof of making a positive effort. We had everything to gain and nothing to lose.

Frequent reports on our successes were made at the board meetings. Many times these updates were provided by our calling officers to give them "air time" with the directors and to help ensure their individual commitment to the program.

Everyone was kept involved and progress was measured and acknowledged continuously. This is an important key to success when trying to focus the efforts of all persons in the organization toward the achievement of a common goal.

The members of the board of directors were asked to open doors with introductions for our calling officers. They were helpful and supportive. Many times they would accompany the calling officer on a sales call or participate in an introductory luncheon. These tactics were important and impressed our prospects.

The directors were recognized for their support and efforts at every board meeting. It was important to acknowledge their contribution, because it was needed on a full time and on-going basis. The more attention we gave them formally and openly, the harder they worked for the bank.

We employed the same technique and motivational accolades that U.S. Army General Omar Bradley gave to General George Patton during the Second World War in the battle for Sicily. He reportedly said: "Give George one headline and he's good for another thirty miles in the attack."

Headlines were given to everyone, our directors, officers, staff, and even our customers who referred business to the bank.

We were definitely in the attack mode, and by the end of 1975 our efforts began to achieve positive results for the bank.

The establishment of a sales culture in any organization is not an easy task. It requires a full time effort on the part of the key executives in the company. It must be the top item on the CEO's agenda and given primary attention in every meeting. It should be the first item in any announcement or discussion with the staff, and be completely obvious to the employees that it has top-of-mind awareness by each member of the management team.

The first question asked at every encounter with any sales representative should be, "What did you sell today?" This simple inquiry will help maintain momentum in the program and let your staff know what is important. And if it's important to you, it should be damned important to everyone in the company.

Another question that should be directed to the employees by management is **"Are you having fun?"**

These inquiring remarks speak volumes about the significant factors that drive organizations to perform well above the norm.

Success, in any new endeavor, ultimately comes after trial and error, but a commitment to the process and a maximum effort by all hands must be emphasized every single day.

As an unknown said, "Selling is like shaving, if you don't do a little bit every day the first thing you know you will be a bum."

Chapter Six
The Unpiggy Bank

First Georgia lost money again in 1975, but compared to the previous year it was a major win. As a matter of fact, most of the banks in Atlanta were doing poorly with the economic malaise hovering over the Southeast and particularly in Atlanta.

At one point during the year, an article appeared in the Wall Street Journal noting the worst performing banks in America. First Georgia Bancshares was on the infamous list with about 30 other institutions. Many of these were large banks in major cities; however, First Georgia was the smallest institution noted on the list.

During that year a bank building caricature, representing Citizens and Southern Bank, appeared on the cover of Forbes magazine with a bright, blood-like stream flowing out the doors and windows. The headline story in the magazine discussed the red ink currently appearing on the bottom line of many banks around the country. Citizens and Southern just happened to receive more graphic notoriety than most of the other institutions.

The banking industry had nowhere to go but up, and by 1976, thankfully, most of the poorly performing institutions were on the road to recovery by the end of the year. A big boost to the improvement was given from the upward thrust of the economy.

First Georgia went 18 consecutive months without a profit. In February 1977, the bank made $8,000. This was a small return on the amount of human and monetary capital that had been invested over the past year and one-half.

But, it was a beginning, after the long dry spell with no joy, before any light appeared at the end of our long tortuous tunnel of recovery.

At the end of the year we posted a net profit of nearly $500,000, which included a capital gain from the sale of an asset. It appeared the bank might finally be on the road to survival. At least, we were hopeful this might be the case.

When 1978 began, we introduced a new advertising campaign in the newspaper displaying First Georgia as the **"Unpiggy Bank."** This limited expense advertising program was developed to position First Georgia as the most economical bank in the Atlanta market, and highlighted the reasonable costs of our services as compared to the other banks in Atlanta.

It was a fun, some said distasteful, primarily our competitors, marketing program. Our graphic newspaper advertisements pictured all the larger banks with the caricature of a pig head on the top of the bank buildings, while little First Georgia hovered below their stately countenance with a welcoming face and the title of the **"Unpiggy Bank."**

The other bankers in Atlanta did not necessarily appreciate our subtle humor with this campaign, but this was war and survival along with market share growth were our goals.

We also continued to emphasize our corporate calling program and made a thrust into the consumer market by introducing a 12 % interest rate, no fee, Master Charge credit card. This was in line with our advertising theme. It was the lowest in the nation at that time and far better than any offering in the local market.

This was our ploy to gain market share. Our base of customers was not as large as the other major banks in the city. We had less to lose and more to gain with this tactic than the competition.

A writer for The Atlanta Journal, Dick Williams, wrote an editorial titled, "Stealing the Moment," which favorably noted First Georgia's position on our no fee credit card. This article appeared when all the major banks in the city announced they would begin charging an annual fee of $12 on their card.

The final sentence in Dick's column summed up our previous advertising program. **"First Georgia calls itself the Unpiggy Bank and that campaign is now passing, mercifully, but with the big banks putting the squeeze on their customers with the new credit card pricing, 'unpiggy' sounds not corny, but true."**

Later in the year, First Georgia advertised a personal line of credit for the consumer customers with a rate tied to the national prime rate. We were the only bank in Atlanta to provide this kind of economical loan pricing.

We also joined the Honest Face check guarantee system. It was provided by my former employer, The First National Bank of Atlanta. This was a bold move as they were a competitor. However, we believed the bank could benefit from this new high-profile service by offering more products to our customers.

A simple interest loan was also introduced and our institution was also the only bank locally to provide this pricing tactic for a consumer installment loan.

First Georgia was the original and only **"Unpiggy Bank,"** and our service menu of products and pricing clearly echoed this claim throughout the Atlanta metropolitan market.

Looking back, these were aggressive marketing tactics in the seventies and eighties. Today, they may not appear as bold as many of these products and pricing techniques have been improved and offered universally in many banking markets. Bankers today are more creative with their advertising and promotion techniques.

But, with all the changes, consolidations, and enhancements in the banking industry, I have not seen or heard of any bank position itself as the **"Unpiggy Bank."** It worked for us because it was an idea, whose time had come, and as Dick Williams wrote in his Atlanta Journal article, "mercifully it passed."

We had another profitable year in 1978. Our earnings were approximately $700,000, representing a 35% increase over 1977.

At the end of the year, Georgia Railroad and Banking Company of Augusta was allowed to convert the $3 million of preferred stock into common stock of the bank. This conversion represented an 80% ownership position of the company. They also paid off the $9 million debt at Chemical Bank.

Our new owners would eventually benefit significantly from our earnings contribution in the years ahead. Also, their stock price would do rather well---meaning their gamble on purchasing the bank and bailing it out ultimately paid-off handsomely.

During the year we added a businesswoman to our board of directors, Mrs. Cecil B. Day, who was Chairman and President of the Cecil B. Day Companies. First Georgia was the first bank in Atlanta to broaden its directorship by including a distaff member.

Mrs. Day was a wonderful choice for our directorate and was most helpful with our Women's Banking Group, which consisted of several very talented ladies in our company. Actually, her husband, Cecil, the founder of Day's Inn, had previously served on the board for several years until his untimely death.

The Women's Banking Department was developed to penetrate this particular business market, promote an awareness of our diversified capability, and broaden our banking position in the full spectrum of the small-to-middle size corporate market.

This group of women bankers became very active in Atlanta, working with women's clubs, business organizations and conducting credit seminars. They were also heavily involved in assisting both women-owned businesses and new corporate start-ups with many of their banking requirements.

The bank created a special niche in this particular market. We developed considerable new business, received high marks for our creativity, and a great deal of positive publicity for being a progressive open-minded organization.

As the sixth largest bank in Atlanta, we realized it was necessary to create "advertising and marketing noise" in order to be noticed in the crowd of "big boys," or the other large banks, by the various customer groups.

We did not have the financial resources to launch any major advertising programs; consequently, we had to live by our wits, so to speak, and do the unusual to bring attention to our company.

We had to out-think and play-off mistakes the other banks made. First Georgia had to be a different breed of bank, a kind of guerrilla, moving through the darkness, taking advantage of its foe when least expected. It was a "hit and run" strategy, and it worked superbly for our small company.

Conventional thinking and actions would not produce the results we needed in the competitive Atlanta market. We were too small and had limited resources. **Thinking, operating and even living outside the box was essential.** This was the only way to survive among a group of excellent and aggressive financial institutions.

This was the same methodology our rifle company used to combat the Viet Cong and North Vietnamese regular army forces in South Vietnam. We were unconventional in our thinking and did the unexpected, actually employing many of the enemy's own tactics against them. We won our little skirmishes, because we didn't go by the book as many fighting units were required to do in their combat zones.

We developed new tactical approaches and makeshift devices to locate the enemy in their hiding places, primarily under ground, catching them off-guard before they could coordinate and launch surprise attacks on our base and troops.

One of our most ingenious weapons, which was mentioned earlier, was a metal spike about four feet long sharpened to a point on one end. It was used by our troops to probe the sandy terrain in our area of operations, as we patrolled and conducted combat sweeps on foot.

We obtained the metal pole, which was about one-third inch in diameter, from used ammo cases containing artillery rounds that were fired from the howitzers at our position. With one end honed like a spear, it made the perfect probe for our use.

With this hand-held device we were able to locate enemy hiding places, booby traps, and arms caches below the surface of the ground, mitigating surprise attacks, and the destructive power of the enemy weapons against our forces.

Our planned tactical movements against the enemy, always executed in an unconventional manner, resembled the old-time movie characters, the Keystone Cops, who seemed to be confused and in disarray when they jumped into action.

We also appeared to be out-of-control with our crazy and "not by the book" tactics as we pursued the enemy, going in multiple directions simultaneously without any apparent rhyme or reason. But, we continuously caught the enemy off-guard with our crazy schemes. However, we knew what we were doing and we did it damned well and won.

Our rifle company was so successful in locating and eliminating the enemy in our zone with our "Mike Spike," the name we fashioned for our probe from our company designation, we were often referred to **as "The Snoopy Poopers."**

We had patches made to wear on our uniforms with the cartoon Snoopy character caring a probe, with a rifle slung over his shoulder, a helmet on his head, cartridge belt around his waist and, of course, a big Marine Corps emblem in the background. Our troops took great pride in their accomplishments, resultant notoriety, and being a member of a highly successful fighting unit.

Success breeds pride in every organization. The more successful, the more pride generated, which normally results in a higher level of performance and accomplishment by all participants.

That same type of creative mentality was put into play with my different banking organizations. We made it a part of our thought process. It touched a chord inside the officers and employees and they accepted and embraced it with enthusiasm. It was fun to be different and maybe even a little crazy. It made our employees proud to know they had a different mentality and persona than the other bankers in the city.

Extensive efforts were made to endear our bank to the press by regularly scheduling luncheons and meetings to talk about banking matters, especially First Georgia's, whenever we could work it into the conversation, which we always managed to do.

When called and asked about any banking issue we always responded. The term "not available for comment" was never considered an appropriate response to the Fourth Estate.

The press appreciated our candor and honesty, but most importantly they appreciated our willingness to indulge them with our time, regardless of the subject matter.

More positive publicity resulted from these actions than any organization could have ever anticipated, and it didn't cost us any money. That was the important issue for the bank. It helped our image and kept our name in the newspaper at the time when we could ill afford the expense of an advertising program.

A series of customer breakfasts were initiated in East Point, Georgia, the location of one of our largest offices, during the Christmas season. These were introduced as a way to thank our customers for their business and to cultivate new prospects. This was a goodwill gesture and a marketing effort to enhance our image and develop more business opportunities.

Normally, we had a prominent speaker address the group with a timely message on political issues or with an economic forecast.

A host of local government figures were invited and naturally they all accepted. It was a great way for them to mingle with their constituents. Carl Sanders and I stood at the entry shaking hands and welcoming each individual personally, while the bank officers moved through the crowd politely and discreetly seeking new business opportunities.

Carl would always introduce all the politicians to the audience, which ensured we would have a great turnout from that contingent. Afterwards, I made some politically observant comments about the bank, updated them on our progress, thanked them for their support, and urged everyone to do more business with us. This was a sales event; there was no pretense otherwise. We were definitely in the hunt for business.

Our keynote speaker would then present his topic for their edification. At the conclusion, each guest left with a small token of our appreciation, a gift for their office, usually inscribed with the bank's name to continuously remind them we were there to help with their financial needs.

Our guest speaker group consisted of some well-known and respected politicians and business leaders, including Mayors Maynard Jackson and Andy Young, Governors George Busbee and Zell Miller, Senator Sam Nunn, Congressman Doug Barnard, and the Presidents of the Atlanta Federal Reserve Bank, Monroe Kimball and Robert Forestall. Joe Torre, the Atlanta Braves manager, also participated while he was engaged with our public relations program.

The noted economist from Georgia State University, Don Ratajczak, who was popular because of his timely forecasts, spoke at our breakfasts on several occasions.

We always had fun with Don, usually introducing him humorously with some disparaging comment about his profession, but he was always quick with a retort after he took the podium.

However, on one particular occasion he was presented with a large glass **"Unpiggy Bank"** filled with shredded money as a token of our appreciation for his fine presentation. He was finally at a loss for words. Don still has the pig and we laugh about it whenever we see each other.

These functions were popular and well received by all of our guests. We always had an amazingly good turnout, many times in excess of 300 people.

The first year, in 1975, we had 75 attendees at the breakfast and the bank had $75 million in assets. The last year of my involvement with First Georgia, during the holiday season of 1985, we had eight customer breakfasts in various locations around Atlanta, with over 2,000 attendees. The bank had grown to nearly $1 billion in assets with nearly $10 million of annual profits.

These events grew to be expensive and time consuming. A few of my executives began carping about the costs. I told the staff, those who did not believe in the power of marketing and advertising, there are always some present in every organization, that we could not afford to discontinue the events.

My rationale presented to these non-believers centered on how much our profits and assets had increased each year since the program was started.

Actually, I was concerned about stopping the breakfasts, even though they were costly, because it might potentially affect our future financial performance. We stayed the course. It is difficult to argue with success.

None of the other institutions in Atlanta were conducting similar events like these for their customers. I was convinced they were instrumental in establishing our unique character and set us apart from the other banks.

The best year in the recent history of First Georgia occurred in 1979, when we made $1 million in profit, a .81% return on average assets, which was a 49% increase over the previous year. Our assets had grown to $130 million, a 15% increase over 1978.

Our balance sheet was strengthened with these earnings and our capital-to-asset ratio was now a respectable 6.88%.

In addition, many of our non-performing loans finally began to show improved performance with the recession ending and loan restructuring we had employed to keep our borrowers afloat.

Our staff had worked diligently with our problem customers during these difficult years. We believed this was the proper course to take, and if we could help them avoid bankruptcy we would derive benefit both as a good community-oriented citizen, and importantly, from their future business.

Actually, we could not afford to charge-off any loans, because it would have severely impacted our earnings and capital. This situation, more or less, dictated the need to be a helpful and understanding lender. This is what bankers should be doing anyway.

Many of these customers did eventually recover from their problems and went on to be successful in the Atlanta business community. As a consequence, these efforts paid-off and we did benefit, as we had hoped in future years.

With the start of 1980, and our increasing profitability, we made plans to begin a branch expansion program by building 5 new offices in the greater Atlanta area. This expansion strategy would extend our reach into the vibrant and growing consumer market and facilitate asset growth.

A new real estate department was opened to take advantage of the recovering Atlanta economy.

An automobile leasing department was started to extend our product reach in both the corporate and consumer markets and to take advantage of the shift in consumer attitude from purchasing to leasing autos.

Russ Bramblet, the owner of the leasing company, had an office in Buckhead, the center of Atlanta, and he and his team of leasing professionals built this department into a major income producing area for the bank.

Our timing was good. Both of these new businesses grew rapidly and were instrumental in helping to extend our profitability into the eighties.

New management talent was injected into some key executive positions, and we increased the number of calling officers at the bank to help promote our business development efforts.

The bank's financial success and frequent appearances in the newspaper, through our efforts with the press, presented an improved image of the bank and we actually had people knocking on our door seeking both employment and banking relationships.

This interest and enthusiasm represented a significant opportunity to bring some highly qualified talent into the organization.

Our primary employment sales pitch centered on two key points: The capability to offer more responsibility to our prospective new employees than many of them had in their current positions, and the opportunity for a faster career path than was normally possible in the typically larger bureaucratic banks.

The current Mayor of Atlanta, Maynard Jackson, was promoting minority business ventures at this time and encouraging banks to add minorities to their board directorate.

He approached First Georgia and inquired about our position on the matter.

I told him he was too late with his inquiry, as we had already made our decision. He then said, "You mean you won't consider my request?" I quickly responded, "No, because we have already done it."

Carl Sanders and I had been discussing the matter for several months and had been looking for a candidate to join our board.

First Georgia served the entire community, and we believed the bank should have board representation from all of our constituents. It just seemed like the right thing to do. We had made a similar decision earlier when we asked Mrs. Cecil B. Day to join our organization.

Tom Cordy, an African-American businessman, who owned AMC Mechanical Contractors, was contacted about his interest in joining the bank board.

After several meetings with Tom, he agreed to our proposal and was unanimously elected by the directorate shortly before Mayor Jackson approached us. We considered ourselves fortunate to have persuaded him to become a member of our growing organization.

He became very active in our business affairs and made significant contributions, as did our other directors to the bank's progress.

Our forward-thinking mentality helped open the door in Atlanta for all classes of minorities to participate more actively in corporate boardroom governance.

Establishing a niche in a business market is not the easiest of tasks to accomplish. Our strategy to concentrate on the small to middle size corporate market produced tremendous results for the bank. We were fortunate that no other financial institution, at that time, had focused their efforts on this businesses segment.

Our capital structure, small size, and position in the market prompted our strategy and decision. Thankfully, we were smart enough to follow through pragmatically with no diversions from this plan.

Management made another critically important decision when we began to focus on our business niche. First Georgia would be a true customer and service oriented institution and this attitude would become an integral part of our culture.

I don't mean to sound naïve, because most banks publicize this approach with their advertising literature. But, many times it is only the application of lip service and not a dedicated operating philosophy of management practiced daily by the bank employees.

Throughout my career in business, especially in banking, it became apparent that the implementation of a sales mentality and customer oriented culture required constant attention and encouragement from senior management. The chief executive must make it a top priority, if it is going to become a way of life and permeate the entire company.

There were no funds available to hire a professional sales training organization. We determined these selling skills would have to be developed over time with an overpowering mindset, a total devotion to the task, and a continuous propaganda effort. We would hire the professionals when we could manage the expense.

We could afford to devote time and energy, but not money, at that stage of our meager existence.

Each time we had a meeting the first item on our agenda would always relate to sales. We always discussed the progress of our sales calling program, and followed this with an analysis on the attention we were providing to our customers.

It was always interesting to try new motivational "tricks" on our staff such as taping a dollar bill to the seats of some of their chairs. During the introduction we would ask everyone to stand and look under his or her chair seats. The unsuspecting employees, who found a dollar bill, would acknowledge their surprise by displaying the money for the entire group to witness. The group would then be asked if they understood the meaning of the exercise.

Without getting much response we would point out the obvious and tell them it was to demonstrate that "you couldn't make a buck sitting on your fanny." In order words, get out on the street and sell products.

Having been active in athletics for many years, I was always impressed with the motivational epithets and slogans the coaches used in practice and hung on the walls to inspire our team on to greater performance. We attempted to follow those same methods with our own staff whenever it was appropriate.

An example, which I liked to use was: "Every day in Africa an antelope gets up knowing it must outrun a lion in order to stay alive. Every day a lion gets up in Africa knowing it must outrun an antelope in order to stay alive. The moral is, it doesn't make any difference if you're a lion or an antelope, but when you get up in the morning, you better get up running."

First Georgia needed employees on the staff, who were **"monomaniacs with a mission."** 1000% insanely dedicated to our programs and objectives. This kind of attitude was essential for our success. It was also an idea whose time had come.

Every person in the bank knew the bank's first priority was selling the products and services. Everything else was secondary.

The future of the company would ultimately materialize from the growth and profits generated as the result of these efforts.

It is common knowledge that the leader should set the pace for an organization. Also, motivation seeps down from the top of an organization, it does not well up from the bottom.

Management of the bank would set the pace and ensure that our staff received all the inspiration on the job they could possibly tolerate.

Another tenet of leadership mentioned earlier, which has probably consumed my thinking for years involved commitment and character.

Do those things you say you are going to do and do them when you say you will. Your life, your job, the existence of your unit or organization may depend on your promise. It should be practiced as an everyday thing not a sometime thing. There should be no excuses for failure to meet one's commitments unless it is caused by an authority outside of our control or not of this earth.

Nothing agitates me more, in today's world, than people failing to follow through on those things they committed to do.

Our thrust in the sales and customer attention areas paid-off handsomely and we began to grow at an accelerated pace.

By the end of 1980, First Georgia had grown to $150 million in assets, a 15% increase or $20 million over the previous year. Net income increased 50% to $1.5 million. Return on assets was a stellar 1.22% on assets, with a 16% return on equity. These financial accomplishments, compared to those of other banks of our size, were considered to be excellent by industry standards.

The Board of Directors was more than happy with the performance of the company. The group had weathered some tough times in the past and had "stayed the course." Their commitment was certainly above and beyond the call of duty, especially considering the bleak outlook for the bank just a few years previously.

New members were added to our directorate to assist us in the marketplace and to enhance the prestige of the company.

At one point we had 30 board members. That was a very large group for a bank our size, however, they were all active in the affairs of the bank and highly effective with our business solicitation efforts.

The large size of our directorate, and their involvement in our solicitation efforts enabled the bank to penetrate more areas of business opportunities than would have been otherwise possible.

According to our chairman, we did have one unknown quantity in the bank. It was the president. I had no standing or recognition in the business community, and no portfolio or following whatsoever, upon joining the company in 1974. But, considering the sad state of affairs at First Georgia, there were probably few, if any qualified bank presidents or senior executives interested in jumping into what looked to be a "sinking ship."

My inexperienced mind saw only opportunity and a chance to build a career when I was interviewed for the position with the bank. Fortunately, that is exactly what it became.

Upon hiring, Carl Sanders had promised I could run my own show. This was my preference and it had a major bearing on my decision. He supported his commitment throughout my 12 years with the company.

While in command of a rifle company in Vietnam, a few years earlier, I had been given the same kind of opportunity. My unit was segregated from the rest of the battalion and assigned its own remote tactical area of operations, several miles distant from any other military unit.

Mandated to operate with limited oversight from any headquarters organization, we were to conduct tactical operations, based on our own assessment of the enemy situation, and provide protection for the Cua Viet River Marine Corps supply base. It was located at the mouth of the river on the South China Sea, a few thousand yards south of the DMZ.

Naval ships would off-load their cargo at this location and it would be taken down river by small boats for distribution to the various units operating in the I Corps area, the northern most sector of South Vietnam.

My other responsibility was to report daily by radio on enemy contacts and provide advance information on our planned combat activities. We were given total flexibility and freedom to formulate our own tactical plans and execute them, as we deemed appropriate.

Our Rifle Company was successful in the engagements with the enemy and received many accolades on our methods, effectiveness, resourcefulness, and most importantly, our results.

Personally, I thrived on the responsibility, authority, and the flexibility of being my own boss, and frankly was probably allowed too much managerial freedom at that time in my life.

A situation like that can do strange things to a person's head; such as causing the development of a superiority complex, belief that you have all the answers, and don't need any senior officer interference. In essence, my own counsel was sufficient. This is not a good practice to follow in war or business.

After growing older and gaining more business experience, those same feelings and desired autonomy became even more important to me. Simply stated, I loved to do things my way. As a consequence of these decisions, many indignities would be cast upon me. This would include some serious ass chewing from my superiors in the business world, because of my neglect to seek their guidance before taking action.

Unfortunately, old habits are hard to unlearn, especially those that are appealing and bring satisfaction and pleasure.

Ultimately, after becoming more moderate with my methods, I was able to abide by at least some of the corporate mandates of my bosses. It was a difficult learning experience and much blood was shed, primarily mine, before reaching this upper plateau of "enlightenment."

This situation was not one managers or leaders should pursue in their careers. Personally, I was fortunate to have survived, particularly after probably "pissing off" most of my seniors with this management approach.

An old quote provides an insight, which if grasped earlier in my life, would have saved me a great deal of anguish and pain.

"If you think you are indispensable, put your finger into a bowl of water, and then remove it and notice the hole that it leaves."

Leaders will not accomplish great things by sitting behind their desks and waiting for others to make decisions or for the solutions to appear mysteriously. They must assert themselves, and if necessary go where the action is to achieve the desired results. This principle should be practiced relentlessly by every individual in a leadership position.

Being a physical and an active person by nature drove me to take a highly involved role in the day-to-day management of the bank, certainly more so than my staff wanted. This also included attending social and political events and making frequent sales calls with my officers.

In my mind, every person contacted was a potential customer of the bank. All Sales people should have this mentality and focus, if they want to reach the pinnacle of success in their field.

Maintaining an active role in the bank's affairs would help my visibility in the community, which Carl Sanders indicated was lacking. It took a great deal of dedication and effort over several years to achieve the recognition that was appropriate for a bank president in the Atlanta market.

Visibility of key management, as well as the company name, is important in the market and is necessary to achieve a top-of-mind awareness with customers and prospects. Recognition of the company promotes a positive feeling among the employees and helps instill pride in the organization. Everyone wants and needs to be acknowledged and identified with success.

There were times when there was too much attention given to me. This situation resulted from our television advertising campaign in 1981.

Our marketing and public relations firm, Howard Skelton and Associates, was managed through our advertising and marketing director, Andrea Strickland. Together, they suggested a more active role as the spokesman for the bank and wanted me to present our advertising messages via television commercials.

They arrived at this recommendation, because no other bank president was visible in the various media markets. I would be the only bank chief executive in the mass media visibly promoting their company.

They assumed this approach would uniquely appeal to the public and reinforce our position as the bank with a human touch.

The concept behind the promotion was to draw comparisons between First Georgia and the larger banks by demonstrating that people, who banked with First Georgia, would receive superior attention and service. Our customers would not be relegated to being an unknown with nothing more than an account number to identify them. In other words, this was a promise from the bank and we would deliver on that guarantee.

Reluctantly accepting their recommendation, we began with my education on how to be a television pitchman. Several commercials were taped at various customer locations to inject realism into our product messages.

We had a moderate budget and ran the television commercials for only a few months. Supposedly, the campaign helped the bank. However, I would not unequivocally admit this resulted from my efforts in the world of television marketing.

The humorous side of this venture concerned the identity confusion created in the market between an automobile dealer in Atlanta and me. He was doing concurrent television ads for his Ford dealership in Decatur, Georgia, suburb of Atlanta.

After we ran our commercials for a few weeks, and later conducted focus interviews with a random sampling of our television audience, we learned there was a good bit of confusion in the viewer's mind between the two of us.

We had similar physical characteristics, such as salt-and-pepper hair, dark complexion, and a quick vocal delivery with our message.

Frequently when in public places I would meet people from all backgrounds (some not too desirable) and they would stop and tell me they had seen me on Tel-E-Vision and wanted to know my name. On many of these occasions they thought I was the car dealer. Perhaps my commercials sold more automobiles than bank services. I don't want too know the answer to that question.

With these embarrassing episodes, we decided my appeal was being misdirected. But, more importantly, we were probably wasting the bank's money.

My illustrious television career was quickly and quietly brought to an anti-climactic end and I vowed never to attempt this again during my business career. Frankly, no one else seemed very interested in trying it again either---thank goodness.

1981 was the best in the company's history. Many of our programs and initiatives were gaining impetus when the year started.

Our staff and employees were now fully trained and committed. They took great pride in their accomplishments and the bank's performance. Each success seemed to promote a higher level of enthusiasm and accomplishment.

When the snowball starts rolling get out of the way and let it roll, but make certain it's going in the right direction.

This was the challenge facing senior management. We had put the correct programs in place, sold them to our team, and they were executing them with a flourish.

They did not need constant supervision, only directional signs placed at critical junction points to keep them moving toward the objective.

Recalling a weekly television program from the eighties starring George Peppard illustrates my point about planning and execution. It appealed to me, because it was an action show and the characters were portrayed as former members of an Army Special Forces Group.

The series was called **"The A Team"** and depicted a four man group of renegade officers, from the Vietnam era, who were then out of the Army and constantly dodging the military police. This occurred because of some alleged wrongdoing perpetrated during the war.

Now, they were dedicated to helping the downtrodden or those being victimized by some bullying group. At the conclusion of each television segment the team won the day by their wits against the bad guys.

The former Colonel, played by Peppard, who had been their leader in Vietnam, headed the civilian team. He would always close the final scene of the show, after they had succeeded with some courageous or crazy scheme with the comment, **"I love it when a plan comes together."**

That is exactly what was happening at First Georgia. Everything we were doing, including all of our plans, were working and coming together nicely.

We opened four new branches in key growth areas in the metropolitan area. This expanded our capabilities to reach more businesses and consumer accounts on the outskirts of Atlanta.

After utilizing the less-than-desirable small basement of the Candler building to house our bank operations group, while our bank was in financial trouble, we could now afford to move this important department into better and more expansive quarters. This step was a strong motivator for our staff.

We leased a building in Atlanta's northeast quadrant close to I-85. It would meet our current needs and provide the capability for our expected growth over the next few years.

These efforts, along with the dedication and attention to our customers; aggressive sales program in the business market, and of course, our plan coming together just like the A-Team, resulted in a spectacular year of financial accomplishments for First Georgia.

Net Income in 1981 increased 36% to $2.3 million with an outstanding 1.43% return on assets. The capital base was increased 19%

to $14.1 million, and return on equity was 19.62%. Total assets increased 20% to $180 million, and total deposits ended the year at $156 million, an 18% increase.

According to Olson Research Associates, a banking industry standards group, assets for all banks grew by 10%, return on assets was .88%, and return on equity was 13.7%.

The **"Unpiggy Bank,"** after experiencing a dismal financial crisis and performance in 1974 and 1975, just like **The fabled Phoenix,** which had risen from the ashes of near destruction, had been resurrected and joined the league of top-performing banks in the country in 1981.

Our progress was similar to that of an U.S. bomber flying somewhere over the Pacific Ocean when the pilot received a radio message from his base requesting their location. He responded, "I have bad news and good news. The bad news is we're lost. The good news is we're making record time."

Chapter Seven
Values

In 1982, one of the most significant events in the history of the banking industry occurred. The Monetary Control Act or the regulation on the rate of interest financial institutions could pay for deposits was changed.

This would also usher in a new wave of interest bearing deposits and permanently alter the asset and liability structure of most financial intermediaries, their funds gathering tactics, and the banking practices of most depositors in the years ahead.

The Money Market Account, introduced by all banks early in the year, was the initial product offering resulting from this regulatory change.

All of the financial institutions in Atlanta were very aggressive with their marketing and pricing of this new product. Every financial organization throughout the country saw this as the vehicle to build their balance sheet and promote new business opportunities.

The competition was particularly robust and crazy in Atlanta. Some of the highest introductory rates in the country would be offered to the depositors in this market during the initial 30-day term.

The banks in Atlanta and around Georgia offered the account with interest rates ranging from 16 to 22%. The rate was only guaranteed for a 30-day period. Afterwards, a market rate would prevail and the new product would be offered strictly on a competitive market basis.

At First Georgia, we concluded this was an opportunity to enhance our market position and decided to introduce our money market account with a rate of 22%. This was the highest paid by any major bank in Atlanta, and if my memory serves me correctly, perhaps the highest across the country.

At First Georgia, introductory premiums such as cameras, radios, binoculars, and clocks were offered as additional inducements to attract customers.

A major part of our marketing efforts included a double-truck, multi-colored newspaper advertisement that was supposed to run for a two-week period in the Atlanta Journal. We believed this would be sufficient to cover the introductory period for this product at our bank.

Our advertising program kicked off one day before the promotion and ran for only two days.

On the first active day of the new deposit product our branches received nearly $90 million in money market deposits, increasing the size of the bank by 35% in less than eight hours.

At the conclusion of the first day of our promotion, it was necessary to discontinue the offering. The bank had taken in more deposits than could be assimilated into its operation. It also created concern about our capital position capability to support this influx of new interest bearing liabilities.

Banks are required to maintain capital-to-asset ratios within prescribed ranges, normally 7 to 10%. These are specified by bank regulations. If capital ratios fall below these limits a bank must raise additional capital by stock offerings, the issuance of capital notes, or other debentures.

After the introduction of the account concluded 30 days later, rates normalized. First Georgia retained over 70% of those deposits generated through the introductory program permanently.

The initial rate was guaranteed for 30 days and then dropped like a rock to 12%. The rate, thereafter, fluctuated based on market conditions, much as it does today, and held in the 7 to 8% range for the remainder of the year.

Although the interest expense associated with our new money market account was exorbitant the first year, over $1 million, these liabilities would fuel the bank's growth for the next two years.

Success is a wonderful thing, but too much, if uncontrolled, can sometimes do more harm than good. We knew we would have to put these funds to work quickly, in either loans or investments, at rates higher than we were paying on these new deposits. Otherwise, the bank would have an imbalance in the interest rate structure, causing a very serious earnings problem that year.

After some quick analysis of our situation, it was decided the most prudent action would be to discontinue the product after the first day. We notified our staff accordingly. However, it was not possible to stop our large advertisements from appearing in the newspapers the next day.

The following morning, before we opened our doors, long lines of people were waiting outside our branches to acquire the new account.

Our branch managers were instructed to inform them, before they came inside our offices, that we had discontinued offering the premium-rate account, and to suggest they quickly go to the nearest competitor's branch.

Most of the people, when they heard the news literally ran out of the parking lots and headed to the nearest bank within sight to invest their funds.

It was a zany time, but most all the banks in Atlanta did very well with this new product. However, none had the kind of success we experienced. Our timing, product promotion, and luck had been perfect.

It is better to be lucky than good and perhaps we had a little of each with our introduction. However, it does seem that most successful people create their own luck.

As a result of the spectacular success of this promotion our assets increased 63% from $180 million to $293 million, and deposits were up 60% from $158 million to $249 million for 1982. Total capital grew 19% to almost $15 million. Net income for the year was up 16% to $2.6 million, and our return on assets was 1.25% for the year. Not a bad performance considering the additional interest and marketing expense we incurred with the money market promotion.

Our financial results were well above the average of banks our size in the industry, according to various bank research groups. First Georgia maintained its position among the top performing banks within this group for the year.

The bank had now grown into the ninth largest commercial bank in the state. In 1975, at the bottom of our troubled period, it was the twenty-second largest in Georgia.

We continued to expand our directorate by adding our second African-American member, Dr. Alonzo A. Crim, Superintendent of the Atlanta Public Schools. Also, the following businessman joined our board. Sidney H. Feldman, President of London Iron & Metal; Wesley E. Cantrell, Jr., President of Lanier Business Products, Inc.; and J. William Travis, Executive Vice President, Southern Bell Telephone.

The bank's other directors, who had stayed the course and happily witnessed the improvement in the company over the previous years were all prominent businessmen in the community and significant contributors to our success.

This group included: Dr. John Atwater, Senior Partner, Internal Medicine Group; Richard A Beauchamp, President, RTC Transportation, Inc.; S. Russell Bridges, Jr., Executive Consultant Georgia International Life Insurance Company; Edward C. Hammond, Vice President (retired),

Georgia Power Company; Jack C. Hodgkins, Partner, Petro Chem Associates; W. Ray Houston, Chairman and President, Fulton County Bank (retired); and James P. Jackson, Partner, Bell, Cowart & Jackson.

The remaining directorate included Graeme M. Keith, Vice Chairman, and Charles B. Presley, Chairman, First Railroad & Banking Company of Georgia; Peter S. Knox, President, Merry Land Companies; T. B. McLeod, President (Retired), Peoples Bank; C. V. Nalley, III, President, Nalley Motors; General Carl T. Sutherland, Personnel Director (Retired), City of Atlanta; General Louis W. Truman, Lieutenant General of the Army (Retired); Dr. William M. Suttles, Provost & Executive Vice President, Georgia State University; and Colie B. Whitaker, Jr., President Whitaker Oil Company and Carl E. Sanders.

All of the members of our board of directors assumed a great deal of responsibility and personal risk during their years of service. They were loyal supporters of the company and provided excellent guidance for management. Words alone can not express the depth of my appreciation for their support and friendship during my 12 years at First Georgia Bank.

Starting in 1983, the Atlanta economy was percolating. Most of the banks in the city had recovered from the past real estate doldrums and were demonstrating positive growth and enhanced earnings. However, the savings and loan industry was beginning to experience severe problems and this situation would continue to worsen for the next several years. The general commercial banking industry was improving its performance rapidly.

Diversification and growth in several new industrial components had begun to materialize in Atlanta; consequently, in the future, there would be less emphasis and reliance on real estate construction lending and land speculation.

This growing business environment would offer increased opportunity for banks to expand their lending into these segments in the future, and not depend on a single market for their lending activities.

First Georgia would benefit from these changes in the economic foundation of the city and conclude the year by again achieving a record earnings level.

Net income for 1983 was $3.4 million, an increase of 32% over the previous year. Assets ended the year at $337 million, an increase of 16%.

The bank's assets had grown rapidly since 1981, as had the earnings. Even with our own capital generation from our ever-increasing earnings, additional funds were needed to support the rapid growth and expanding operations.

Our parent, now called First Railroad and Banking Company of Georgia, previously named Georgia Railroad Bank of Augusta, had formed a new holding company and was called on to infuse capital notes of $1.5 million to support our continued expansion and growth objectives. They now owned 100% of First Georgia Bank, and First Georgia Bancshares was no longer operative as the Holding Company of the bank.

Atlanta was and is still a dynamic market. When considering our location in this expanding city and progress of the bank during past few years, it was a relatively easy discussion to convince our owners of the wisdom to provide the additional funds.

Our return on capital was 24% in 1983 and had averaged 24.69% over the previous five years. Our compound growth rate in assets had also averaged over 24% for the past five-year period.

Capital Infusion was a no-brainer when it became obvious we needed more in order to continue to grow and contribute increased profits to the corporation.

If a management team is aggressive and adventuresome they should always be looking for better ways to accomplish the company's objectives.

Stored away in my aging yellowed notes is a quote by an unknown writer that makes this point explicitly:

"What was once good soon ceases to be good, because something better is always possible."

In keeping with this point we began looking for new tricks that would be beneficial in meeting the competitive challenges ahead. The Bank had to continue to grow and maintain its earnings momentum in order to remain viable and contribute positively to the performance of our parent, First Railroad.

Acquisitions were one of the vehicles we could ride, but we were not quite ready to assimilate any new operations into our core fabric---just yet.

Early in 1983, I decided to enroll in an Outward Bound course in North Carolina, thinking this kind of training might be useful to the bank's managers and help improve teamwork, espirit de corps, and risk-taking within the company.

My previous background in the Marines obviously played into this decision. Knowing how physical challenges had helped mold people in the Corps into viable, supporting, and cohesive units, I reasoned a similar type of training might be helpful for our staff and could significantly influence our culture.

My chief financial officer, Jim Box, who had been with the bank for several months and was a strong proponent, would accompany me on this adventure. He was more than willing to go and was excited about using this training method to further improve First Georgia Bank's performance.

Since leaving the Marines in 1968 I had not slept in the outdoors or participated in any outside activities except for jogging and tennis. It would be a personal challenge for me to undertake this program, but the experience was necessary in order to evaluate it properly for our bank.

After fifteen years of living the soft life as a civilian, I was anxious to get back to the challenge of surviving in the woods and to re-open those early pages of my past life's book.

Jim had not been active in wilderness programs up to this time. Consequently, our involvement would serve similar introductory purposes for both of us, while we evaluated it as a potential training tool for our management team.

When we enrolled in the Outward Bound mountaineering program we did not realize those nine days in the mountains, under severe winter weather and physically demanding conditions, would alter our personal lifestyles forever.

The challenge of developing our field-craft skills, living with the bare essentials in the woods, and the physical stress on our bodies, coupled with the exhilarating risk-taking exercises, eventually cast us in a role of permanent "adrenaline junkies."

From that day forward, after completing the course, we would constantly find ourselves seeking new physical adventures for a mental high. We became addicts to these demanding programs, ultimately spending a large amount of our future vacation time engaged in similar activities.

After completing that initial course, we subsequently enrolled in other Outward Bound programs including mountain climbing in Colorado, canoeing in the Everglades and Okefenokee Swamps, hiking and rock climbing in the high desert of the Joshua National Forest in California, and rafting wild rivers in Utah, Tennessee, and Georgia.

The bank's attorney and partner with Troutman Sanders, Mack Butler, who had been responsible for managing and coordinating all our legal issues throughout our difficult times, was also an avid outdoorsman and joined us on most of these odysseys.

After completing a half-dozen courses the three of us started planning our own adventure trips, and would arrange our vacation schedules to allow us to take two each year, mostly to the western states.

These were great stress relievers, however, we would normally return from these trips in a semi-exhausted physical state.

My secretary, Joy Day, said we "looked like death warmed over and totally ragged out" when we arrived back at the office. But, our minds would be much clearer, free of clutter, and ready for the "whatever might come" challenges of our work environment.

That initial Outward Bound Program was a life-altering experience. It not only positively changed much about our lives and interests, but also influenced our decisions in running the company.

We concluded from our initial experience that the use of programs like Outward Bound in our management-training syllabus would help develop a much stronger, self reliant, and decisive group of leaders in the bank.

Paradoxically, upon completion of the course and return to the bank, we decided not to use Outward Bound in the training program for the company.

We believed it might be too strenuous and overwhelming for some of our managers. We did not want to discriminate between the staff members who could physically meet the standards and those who could not.

The nine-day course time frame was also a barrier. It would be difficult to schedule large groups of managers to participate for such an extended period.

It was necessary to find another program to accomplish our team-building objectives, allow us to enroll more of our managers, and make people feel they had been challenged, but not put through a survival training course.

Although this program did not fit our bank's objective, it was a great teaching vehicle conducted by professionals. Any organization seeking to improve the quality of its management team would be advised to consider this program for team building and value-add leadership improvement.

In the interim, while continuing our search for the most suitable program, we scheduled several white-water rafting trips for groups of 40 managers. It was anticipated these exposures could also help cement our team into a stronger and more cohesive group.

On several early Saturday mornings we would depart by bus to either the Chattooga River in north Georgia or the Nantahala River in North Carolina for a day of team building and physical challenge.

Our managers, grouped in teams of six to a boat, then battled and paddled their rafts across the swirling waters of these gushing wild rivers for six hours. We concluded the day with a steak cookout and a few beers, arriving back in Atlanta late in the evening physically spent.

Everyone had a great time. They learned more about working together, while they shared in the physical labor of rowing and maneuvering their unforgiving rubberized craft in the white-water, while it crashed about the river-laden rocks.

The beer and steaks, after the adventure, helped mitigate the strain from the day. Everyone was usually quite mellow by the time we boarded the bus for home in an almost exhausted state.

The movie Deliverance was shown on the bus en-route to the Chattooga River to help prepare them for this new adventure. It was filmed in the same locale where we conducted many of our river experiences. It helped induce some increased amount of lively anticipation for the experience.

The time spent together provided our staff with the opportunity to get to know each other better, under some extreme conditions, while sharing a common bond through their participation in this physically demanding event.

They were being indoctrinated for more challenging training. The river exercise was a great introduction and helped soften the initial exposure and anxiety for the next phase of outdoor training yet to come.

Later that year, we located the program that would meet our needs. We contracted with Executive Challenge, a unique award-winning outdoor management and professional development-training program sponsored by Boston University's School of Management. It was operated locally by the Atlanta based Executive Adventure Group.

The program normally ran for three rigorous days in a remote area, where our managers would be sequestered from interruptions and could fully "enjoy" their time away in the woods.

This method provided them the time to fully concentrate on their involvement in the program and "enjoy" every minute.

Bob Carr and his highly trained staff operated the Executive Challenge program. It provided a blend of outdoors-physical problem-solving activities, including the treetop ropes obstacle course. Carr's team of professional instructors, after each initiative, conducted discussions and debriefings, reviewing the management principles employed by each group of participants.

The managers were required to explore the elements of teamwork and trust with these activities and to improve their ability to communicate, take risks, solve problems, and confront personal challenges---qualities essential to good leadership and management.

When these programs were initiated in late 1983, we were on the leading edge of management training with this educational technique. Later, a number of larger corporations gravitated toward the outdoor management-training technique, and it ultimately received a great deal of notoriety and acceptance in the corporate world.

First Georgia utilized the training method in its early introduction period and enrolled over 250 key personnel in the program during a three-year period.

At the conclusion of each course, we would debrief the participating group on their experience and ask them to review with their team members what they had learned. This follow-up technique demonstrated management's interest and enthusiasm for the training.

One particular learning experience cited by a woman branch manger, during the debriefing, demonstrates the value of this training and is worthy of repeating.

She related the difficulty she had crossing a rope suspended between two trees, fifty feet above the ground.

It was part of the "ropes course." It included several different initiatives performed above ground on tree suspended ropes. Of course, all of the participants had safety attachments affixed to them to preclude injury in the event they miscued.

She told the group that as she pulled her middle-aged body along the horizontally suspended rope high in the trees, she didn't think she had the strength or courage to make the 50 feet of distance she was required to traverse. But, she was determined and finally completed the obstacle after taking nearly twice the time of her teammates.

Furthermore, she noted she would not have made it through the challenge if it not been for her fellow officers urging and cheering her on from the ground below. They served as both her mental safety net and support group.

She was asked what she learned from her experience and how could she use it in her job. She responded; "I learned I need to be more of a cheerleader for my people. With this kind of moral support and encouragement they could probably accomplish any task given to them."

A graduation ceremony was conducted at the end of each program. All participants were presented with a framed camouflaged colored certificate encircled with a small knotted rope. They were asked to display these unusual plaques in their offices for all their employees and customers to view.

It was anticipated our officers would take great individual satisfaction in their achievement, while realizing few people, especially bankers, had ever completed or much less even attempted such a challenging and demanding training program.

The personal pride each individual exhibited upon completion of the course was overwhelming, as was the surge of enthusiasm that spread throughout the bank. The pride in their individual accomplishments was contagious among all of the employees.

This particular training became part of our culture and provided the bank with a personality and status few companies could claim in the business world.

We were referred to in some local publications as the **"crazy Atlanta bankers who swing from trees."** I thought it was a complimentary and fitting accolade for our staff.

Tom Peters, the noted author and business guru wrote in his book, Liberation Management, published in 1992; "If you don't feel a little crazy, you're just not in touch with the times." He also wrote: "Dull leaders for dull times. Zany leaders for zany times."

At First Georgia we tried to be both zany and crazy, and probably achieved these goals most of the time.

In 1982, Peters co-published his first book with Robert Waterman Jr., also with McKinsey & Company, **In Search of Excellence: Lessons from America's Best-Run Companies.**

The book became an instantaneous success and was the top management best seller in the United States for over a year. Five million copies were purchased by 1992.

In Search of Excellence reviewed eight basic business practices that Peters and Waterman discovered in their lofty research. These were defined as the operating characteristics of successfully managed companies. They are worthy of review and are still timely.

1. **A bias for action, for getting on with it.** A corporate preference for action.

2. **Staying close to the customer**. These companies learned from the people they served, while providing unparalleled service for their customers.

3. **Autonomy and entrepreneurship.** Their employees were encouraged to think and act independently.

4. **Productivity through people.** The employees were valued as the root source of quality and productivity.

5. **Hands-on, value driven.** There was a corporate requirement that all the executives keep in touch with the firm's essential business.

6. **Stick to the knitting.** Primary attention and focus was given to the business the company knew best.

7. **Simple form, lean staff.** Only a few administrative layers containing a small number of people were maintained at the upper levels.

8. **Simultaneous loose-tight properties.** These companies were both centralized and decentralized. They pushed autonomy down in the organization to the rank and file.

Reading the book in early 1983, I was overwhelmed with the authors' findings and insights into the management process. They had committed to writing and explanation many of the same attributes we had been trying to implement at First Georgia.

Jim Box, my CFO, and I attended a seminar in the latter part of the year given by Tom Peters in Princeton, New Jersey. It was hosted by the Young President's Organization, of which I was a member. After hearing Peters' presentation we immediately jumped on his bandwagon.

Peters primarily reviewed the eight principles noted in the book. He also discussed corporate value systems, an issue more in need today in corporate America than in 1983, because of the recent corporate misconduct manifested in some companies.

We took copious notes and were particularly interested and impressed with his value system discussion. We immediately began to think about how we might implement a value statement at First Georgia. By the time we arrived in Atlanta, after the three-day presentation, we had completed a draft containing our thoughts and beliefs.

After finalizing the document, it was printed, routed throughout the company, and placed in conspicuous locations for all our employees and customers to view.

We emphasized to the staff the need to become totally familiar with these guidelines, because they would be adhered to in all future activities of the bank. Also, we wanted our customers to be aware of the practices that were to be routinely employed at the bank.

We also informed the staff that there would be follow-up instruction and training on the principles noted in the book.

All of our managers were encouraged to read the publication. A supply of the books were purchased and made readily available. Everyone understood this was a priority.

After that introduction, we had an enthusiastic response and acceptance. It was made clear there was no other acceptable alternative. The statement follows:

First Georgia Bank Company Values

**A customer attitude that promotes friendly,
courteous and dedicated service.
A learning atmosphere that allows our staff
to grow into the best they can be.
An encouragement toward innovation, so as to
challenge us and our competitors.**

**A financial reward system, which recognizes
performance and contributions to corporate goals.
An organizational environment in which
employees can have fun performing their work.
A devotion to integrity in all business
transactions and relationships.
A corporate commitment in meeting
our social responsibilities.**

In mid-1984, my education on this subject was further advanced, while attending my first "Skunk Camp" with 40 other dedicated stalwarts from various companies.

The Palo Alto Consulting Group, a company founded by Tom Peters, sponsored this program. This organization was chartered to focus its activities on serving a small number of corporations with management training. It later developed into a major consulting firm hosting workshops and seminars around the country.

The **Skunk Camp** was designed to bring people together to swap stories about their successes with the **In Search of Excellence** practices. Interestingly, many of the people in attendance or their companies had been mentioned in the book.

The **Skunk Camp** or **"Skunk Works"** term and practice was initiated by the Lockheed Company. It denoted a highly innovative, fast-moving, and slightly eccentric activity or group of people operating at the edges of their corporate structure in problem solving.

After attending this informative program and meeting these devoted practitioners of business excellence, the next step for First Georgia, in its quest for excellence, became abundantly clear.

The bank would bring members of the Palo Alto Group to Atlanta and have them conduct similar seminars for our managers.

Bob Le Duc, a colleague of Tom Peters, would head up the assignment, and true to my commitment to provide more management training on this subject, we began these programs a few months later.

Le Duc conducted six seminars. Each one ran over a three-day period, and over three hundred people were trained on the Excellence concepts in our own "Skunk-Type" sessions.

At the conclusion of each seminar, a critique was conducted with the attendees and they discussed what they had learned. Collectively, each group would then develop action items for the bank or team to pursue over the next several months.

There was to be no communication failure on the agreed course of action.

The goal preached, as usual, was "to do what you say you're gonna do when you say you're gonna do it." They were tired of hearing my sermons about commitment, but they continued anyway. Our officers knew the subject material was important to me and they probably reasoned it should also be important to them.

I had a copy of Peters and Waterman's book wrapped in brown Manila paper with the inscription, **"The Bible,"** printed in bold black letters on the front cover. This was carried with me to many of our staff meetings to reinforce my intentions, their follow-up actions, and to ensure clarity of purpose.

Frequently, when in front of the group, I would open it and turn to a specific chapter and read a comment to help drive home my point. It was a dramatic gesture, but everyone understood.

Since my early days of training in the Marine Corps, I had not personally experienced as much exuberance and enthusiasm for a subject.

This material would be used extensively during the remaining years of my business career. Two years later, after joining Georgia Federal, we would implement similar programs for the management and staff of that institution.

I had a strong inclination, throughout my life in management and in leadership positions, towards the **"bias for action"** principle, although I had never heard that term used to describe the decision process. The opposite of this principle is obviously **"paralysis through analysis,"** meaning lots of studying and evaluating with little or no action initiated.

In the Corps, we were taught to gather our information, evaluate it quickly, as time was always critical, and make a decision based on our knowledge and training. Afterwards, we were instructed to be decisive in our actions and get the job done in the allotted time frame.

It is also my belief that the utilization of personal intuition is an excellent source to influence or facilitate a decision. Of course, intuition comes with experience, doing your homework, and having a sense or knowledge of the battlefield or marketplace about you.

There were times during contact with the enemy in Vietnam when we were required to make an intuitive judgement and subsequent decision on our tactics and direction of attack. Many times this process provided an advantage for us against our foe.

What inner source drives or guides the intuitive judgement of most successful people? The answer to the question is difficult to comprehend. It must be the result of experience, knowledge, acquired skills, and personal confidence gained through years of training and practice. This in turn must feed the intuitive processes of the active mind. Perhaps, a little luck also fits into the equation, but then we frequently create on own luck with decisiveness, a committed effort, and rapid action.

Even though the **"bias for action"** principle appealed to me and I used it extensively to make a point throughout my banking career. I must admit that some of the results from this decision preference were better than others.

Whenever a miscue did occur, meaning a bad judgement was made using this process, I would tell myself a person couldn't be right all the time, regardless of their intelligence quotient.

Another phrase used by Peters and Waterman to describe this alleged management principle was, **"Ready, Fire, Aim."**

This term was more appealing to me than a **"bias for action,"** when speaking or cajoling my staff about accomplishing objectives with short deadlines.

Hell, I knew we would make some mistakes so why not get on with the job, and correct them later. At least we would initiate momentum and it would help keep everyone on his or her toes.

It was my belief that we knew enough about our jobs, the market, and the competition to use our initiative and intuition. I was confident our enthusiastic approach would ultimately result with success in almost any endeavor undertaken.

At our Christmas dinners, later at Georgia Federal Bank, which were hosted each year for our senior officers to acknowledge their accomplishments, they were presented with a present from Santa Claus. Frequently, he was a "jolly" and somewhat rotund Durwood Fincher, the noted corporate speaker and humorist, Mr. Doubletalk, wonderfully masquerading as St. Nick.

At one such affair, Judy Horton, our marketing director, had arranged for a surprise gift to be given to me by Mr. Claus. Opening the package I found a copy of Tom Peter's new book, **Thriving on Chaos, A Handbook for Revolution.**

There was a slight alteration to the book's cover. It had been reworked and was freshly wrapped in bright gold paper with the following inscription on the front: **Creating Chaos by Keeping Your Management Team Off Guard and On Goal, by Richard D. Jackson, Master of Ready, Fire, Aim.**

It was the perfect sentiment for a "**monomaniac with a mission.**"

All of these "crazy stunts" were important for the bank's continuing performance. During the previous years we had brought an abundance of new people on board and everyone had to adapt to this culture, if we were going to maintain our momentum.

Throughout the year we continued our expansion program by opening three new offices and acquiring the Capital City Bank of Hapeville, Georgia. It had $24 million in assets and two branches. The time had finally arrived and we were prepared to initiate an acquisition and merger strategy.

Our advertising agency, Cargill, Wilson, & Acree recommended we hire the Atlanta Braves baseball manager, Joe Torre, as a public relations spokesman for the bank.

Joe had only recently moved to Atlanta, assumed his new managerial position, and the Braves had started the year with a 19 game winning streak.

He was very popular, articulate, friendly, and seemed like the perfect choice to help with our public relations and marketing efforts in the city. He was a likeable person and we became good friends. Joe was extremely supportive of our efforts and participated in our branch openings, meeting and greeting customers, in our advertising programs, and as a special guest at all of our social functions. He was a terrific asset and was well received by our customers whenever he made an appearance.

There is an old quote that reads; "When the wind stops blowing start rowing." At First Georgia we had our oars in the water all the time and had to paddle like hell most of the time.

Chapter Eight
Transition

First Georgia started 1984 full of "piss and vinegar." We had a strong economy and an inspired group of employees, who knew and understood what needed to done. They did it and produced an outstanding year at the bank.

Earnings increased 47% over the previous year from $3.4 million to $5 million. Return on assets was 1.31% and return on equity was 24.43%. Total assets expanded by $110 million to $448 million.

It was a truly an exceptional performance by the bank and we maintained our status as a top performing bank within our industry group.

At the beginning of the year we moved our main office and all of our headquarters facilities from the historic Candler Building on Peachtree Street to a newly constructed and prestigious building at 55 Park Place. It was only one block from our current offices.

The relocation of our headquarters and main office was prompted by a leasing rate increase that we believed to be out of proportion to the market and much too costly for a lessee, who had been a prompt paying client for a number of years. We paid the lease payments when we couldn't pay some of our other bills.

Our landlord thought he had us over the perennial barrel when he announced the increase and would make no concession whatsoever on the rate. Finally, he told us we couldn't move, even though our lease was up for renewal, because it would be too expensive and deleterious to our reputation and ability to service our customers.

That was all the warning and advice needed from him. Within two weeks we had worked–out an arrangement with the leasing agents at Park Place to move. In a short 60 days we were recent history in the Candler Building.

The owner, a former Navy captain, who actually resided in California couldn't believe how quickly we acted or that we would seriously consider moving to another location.

He was left in a very difficult situation and was unable to lease the vacated space for some time. We could have cared less.

Actually, he did FGB a favor. Our new location was much better, more accessible, prominent, and provided the bank a higher level of visibility and stature in the city. Our customers matriculated to the new branch easily and without any complaint.

There was an important lesson, as a former career military officer that he should have recalled from his Navy training.

Never tell anyone they can't do something, because it's just not practical or unrealistic. In the end, if committed, they may surprise you and accomplish the impossible.

Actually, there is a Marine Corps slogan that is more to the point. It probably defines the best attitude about getting things done in a critical time frame, regardless of the circumstances.

"The possible we do today. The impossible takes a little longer."

Much of the training we had accomplished with our staff was paying nice dividends in the form of enhanced individual performance; otherwise, we would not have experienced the great year.

The employees were offered three training experiences, on the average, annually. Of course, this does not include the vast number of employee and sales meetings we conducted to keep our team focused on our primary objectives---sales, growth and profits.

A locally operated Mystery Shopper program was used as a tool to evaluate our sales effectiveness, customer service, and to critique any branch weaknesses.

Once each quarter we had the mystery shoppers, professionals disguised as prospective customers, visit our branches, open accounts, and conduct various transactions. They would evaluate our teller's performance, our new account personnel's knowledge, and grade the branch housekeeping.

The Mystery Shopper reports were submitted shortly after the visit and each manager was required to review the findings with their office personnel.

The information served as a scorecard on performance and everyone in the branch was always concerned about how they were rated. It was a teaching tool and not a disciplinary

method. The program was implemented to help us focus on the attention we were providing our customers and how they perceived our banking knowledge and willingness to provide superior service.

During the year we implemented another zany initiative to help maintain our focus on customer service. We installed three clear glass fishbowls in customer prominent locations in all our branches.

Each bowl had a single word printed on the front in bold letters: **fair, good,** or **excellent.**

Beside each bowl was placed a small jar of large, clear marbles and a sign containing the message; **"Please tell us how you liked our service by placing a marble in the appropriate container."**

After a customer completed their transaction with one of our branch representatives they were asked to grade the service by placing a marble in the chosen container.

Daily we had an official "marble count" submitted by each branch, which more or less quantified the customer's view of the service level at that point in time.

We had fun with the program, as did our customers, and the branch staff took great pride in the results, if they had favorable responses from their daily "fishbowl vote."

Our employees demonstrated a high level of personal interest in their perceived service ranking, and would frequently watch the customer make their choice as they dropped the marble in the selected bowl upon departing the branch.

Immediate positive response for good individual performance is a strong motivator for most people and helps maintain their focus on the objective.

The goal established for "all hands" was to achieve the highest customer service level of any bank in Atlanta, and to get the recognition from the people who mattered, our customers, to back up the claim.

A leader's continuing attention on the important corporate issues determines the priorities for a company. Ultimately, this will establish the character and define the performance of the organization.

With the many training and motivational techniques used to promote results, superior performance was anticipated from all our staff and we were more than willing to pay for it.

Twenty-five different incentive programs were put into operation throughout the First Georgia organization. Every employee had the opportunity to benefit financially from his or her extra efforts and contributions above the norm.

Each financial award, when presented to the employees, was accompanied with specially designed achievement medals denoting their accomplishment. The more we acknowledged, recognized, and rewarded them for their dedication, the more effort and commitment they made toward achieving higher levels of performance.

The enthusiasm fed on itself and the snowball got larger as it rolled down the hill. All that management had to do was to learn to get out of the way. This was Basic Motivation 101 and it works every time.

Continuing and frequent personal recognition is a critical part of the foundation for motivation and always results in improved individual performance.

A box was leased at the Fulton County Stadium to entertain our customers at football and baseball games. Our account officers were to ensure we filled the 24-seat box to capacity at every game played at the stadium.

The customers loved the attention and we treated them royally with food and libations at each event. This provided an opportunity for new business prospecting, customer recognition, and the development of stronger business relationships.

There were times when we had over 50 people in attendance. With a seating capacity of only 24 spaces and a group that size, "we could get real close to our customers."

Everyone always had a great time, regardless of the number of guests. I always thought the more the merrier, but not everyone may have had the same feeling. Nevertheless, our customers always went away with positive feelings about the bank and our calling officers, who were genuinely interested in their customers.

Durwood Fincher, Mr. Doubletalk, our own errant Santa Claus from time to time, who has now achieved fame as a humorous corporate speaker, worked the bar and handled most of the logistics for our box. He also kept everyone in "stitches" with his funny comments. He was a great friend of the bank and enjoyed the camaraderie of both our officers and guests.

We hosted a Customer Appreciation Day every year, sometimes in conjunction with Halloween, to acknowledge and provide a special thank you to our customer base.

The branch employees would dress in costumes, appropriately decorate the offices, and provide apples, cider, and cookies for all the people, who visited the office.

They wore special badges with the words, "I love My Customer," and placed customer appreciation day banners both inside and outside the branches.

We mailed invitations to our customers by putting them into the monthly checking and savings account statements. There was always a great turnout for these events, as evidenced by the number of apples we gave away each year. Our records indicated we used over 30,000 large Virginia apples at this event.

Three of our directors would tour the branches and award prizes for the best costumes and branch decorations. It was a fun day and the customers and employees had an enjoyable time.

No other bank in Atlanta, to my knowledge, conducted this type of celebration. The event served as another distinct opportunity for us to differentiate First Georgia, in a pleasurable way, from the other financial institutions.

During the summer months we encouraged all of our personnel to wear T-shirts to work on Fridays. This was normally the busiest banking day of the week.

Every year a colorful and decorative shirt was designed with the bank's name on the front or back, along with our current advertising theme. One was given to every employee to wear for special events.

The staff enjoyed dressing differently, and our customers appreciated the human character exhibited by First Georgia.

The shirts were very popular, almost becoming a collector's item, and we used them as gifts whenever we hosted some type of customer program. The idea was "corny," but it got us attention, and everyone always seemed to appreciate the gesture.

During my twelve years at First Georgia and seven at Georgia Federal, probably 100,000 T-shirts were given to our employees and customers.

To this day, I still see people wearing these shirts while jogging or working out.

The old adage someone coined, probably in a ridiculous situation, sums up our attitude about many of the things that we tried at First Georgia and Georgia Federal. **"If it's stupid but works, it ain't stupid."**

We frequently had customer surveys conducted by independent research organizations to test our image. According to the participants, First Georgia's banking persona did not match with the typical characteristics often used to describe other financial institutions.

When the people participating in the survey were asked to give their impression of First Georgia, we were never identified as stogy, old fashion, or conservative. People familiar with the company and our advertising viewed the bank as upbeat, creative, youthful, and different from the other banks.

Most all of our crazy "stunts" seemed to ingratiate our employees with the customers, providing us with a truly unique personality and reputation, which set us apart from the "maddening crowd" of the other financial institutions.

We continued our expansion program and new product introductions by installing Automated Teller Machines in some of our branches and offering trust services for both individuals and corporations.

In keeping with our old "Unpiggy" advertising theme we introduced a new consumer checking account, Momentum checking, with the highest interest rate in the city and no monthly fee. Few banks offered totally free checking in those days.

We were fortunate to have had First Financial Management as our provider of computer services during my years at First Georgia. The company, headed by Pat Thomas, gave us great support and was highly reactive to our needs. Without their assistance we would not have had the ability to introduce so many different products, substantially improving our ability to compete.

A second businesswoman, Betty R. Smulian, joined our directorate early in the year. Mrs. Smulian was the Chairman of the Board and owner of the Trimble House Corporation; a Norcross based lighting fixtures company.

Mrs. Smulian worked diligently, along with Mrs. Dean Day, to help maintain the growth and activities of our Women's banking department.

During the year I became involved with the Atlanta Council of the United Service Organizations, USO, and undertook this opportunity with a great enthusiasm.

I served as president of the council for three years at the urging of Mary Lou Austin, who was the executive director. She and her staff were extremely well respected in the community for their efforts. They served a noble purpose in providing needed assistance to our military personnel and their families.

My military background influenced this desire to become involved with this organization. I had enjoyed and appreciated the various USO activities and shows, while in the Marine Corps and away from home during some personally sad holiday seasons.

The Atlanta office did a great job assisting the families and active duty military personnel when they were travelling or relocating to new duty stations. The USO also provided much-needed help to the military dependents, when their spouses were deployed, at critical times with various out-reach assistance programs.

My involvement was a way to give something back for the assistance they rendered to our men in uniform, and for the support experienced while a member of the Armed Forces.

First Georgia continued emphasizing the Executive Adventure and Excellence in Business programs for our staff. Arrangements were made for Tom Peters, personally, to visit our organization and conduct presentations on the material in his book, **In Search of Excellence**.

Tom's enthusiastic and knowledgeable lectures were always well received by every audience. His experienced insights and research data from his work with numerous companies provided the listener with a great deal of instantly usable take-away information.

It was important to have him visit First Georgia, because we had a number of challenges to face. Our staff could use all the inspiration, new ideas, and encouragement we could muster for the coming year.

Our parent company, First Railroad and Banking Company, had been busy acquiring banks in Georgia and now owned three other commercial banks, in addition to First Georgia, in the general Atlanta area.

Gwinnett County Bank and Trust, The Commercial Bank of Cobb County, and The Commercial & Exchange Bank of Bremen, Georgia had all been purchased in recent years.

When 1985 began, a decision was made to merge these institutions with First Georgia.

This would allow the surviving company, First Georgia Bank to take advantage of the synergies, cost savings, marketing opportunities, and advertising leverage for all the institutions under the most identifiable name. The combined size and scale would not only enhance our image in the market, but would facilitate growth in assets and profits more rapidly in the long run.

The combined assets, of the three new banks, were $260 million. First Georgia's assets totaled $450 million when the consolidation process started. Earnings from the three acquired banks had been $2.9 million the previous year compared to $5 million for First Georgia.

During the previous year much of our time had been devoted to assimilating the Bank of Hapeville into our operations. The conversion of these three banks simultaneously into a single operating entity would be more challenging, requiring a major commitment of our management effort over the next 12 months.

The acquisition of a company is not overwhelmingly difficult, assuming the buyer and seller can agree on a price. The problem is making it work afterwards. The integration of new people, policies, corporate politics, and egos can be debilitating and time consuming, even when you own the organization.

We were required to address these issues and the loss of some key personnel, who had no desire to make any change in the way they had conducted business prior to the merger.

Human chemistry has always been an interesting study for me. It is fascinating how people, from different organizations, who are in the process of a sale/purchase transaction can seemingly work together until the money actually changes hands. Afterwards, when the acquisition or merger has been completed, at least on paper, and the organizations are in the process of being physically combined the situation seems to resemble a cartoon I saw several years ago.

One of the characters was asking some people if anyone knew what the Polish workers' union slogan was. Someone in the crowd responded: "Yes, it's every man for himself."

Unfortunately, this comment is probably more accurate in the business context than we would like to admit. However, there is one rule that should be adhered to in the purchase of any organization by another and that is **follow-up.**

Once the due diligence has been performed, synergies and cost reductions determined and plans finalized, get on with the integration process immediately. The longer the time lapse after the deal is done, the more difficult and time-consuming it will be to inculcate a new mindset, operating philosophy, and the other desired changes in the acquired company.

This was our game plan and we moved forward with it as soon as the decision was announced to consolidate the banks. This would increase the number of our branch locations to over 40. The network of offices was spread over several counties around Atlanta.

The merger of the four banks ultimately progressed relatively well, after all the gnashing of teeth, management aggression, and distracting "but we have always do it that way" issues were resolved.

The new First Georgia ended the year 1985 with assets of $851 million and net income of $9.8 million for the combined operations.

On a consolidated basis, assets had grown $141 million or 20%, and net income had expanded $1.9 million or 23.5%. The return on assets was a stellar 1.30%, and return on equity was 22.5%.

The decision to merge these banks had proven to be financially sound, as evidenced by the performance of the combined companies. It had also given much greater prominence and recognition to the First Georgia name in the metro Atlanta market.

Our board of directors was expanded, as a result of the consolidation and we added six new directors from the three merged institutions.

John E Aderhold, President, Rayloc Division of Genuine Parts Company; Otis A. Brumby, Jr. President and publisher, Marietta Daily Journal; A. D. Little, President, Little & Smith, Inc.; Walton K. Nussbaum, the new President of First Railroad & Banking Company of Georgia; Warren P. Sewell, Jr.; President Warren Sewell Clothing Company, and R. Steve Tumlin, personal investment consultant.

We also added two new members to our management team, Edward Milligan, President of the Commercial Bank of Cobb County, and Grady Coleman, President of Gwinnett Bank & Trust.

All of the boards of the acquired banks were dissolved as soon as the consolidation was completed.

During the seventies and eighties many acquiring institutions would attempt to maintain the directorate of the acquired organizations as honorary or advisory directors for goodwill reasons.

I had the dubious task of conducting meetings for these groups in three different banks for a period of time. This practice was time consuming, costly, unproductive and totally without merit.

All of the former directors of these banks were fine, upstanding individuals in their community. However, once they were removed from the liability associated with a directorship and the responsibility of providing policy guidance to management, their interest and enthusiasm declined considerably, which is not uncommon and should be expected in most circumstances.

Once an organization is acquired, it is far better to remove all the past and non-essential associations of the acquired company and follow your own game plan and working arrangements. Hopefully, this can be accomplished with the concurrence and support of all parties. These are politically tough decisions, but they need to be made with no pretense other than it is in the best interests of the surviving organization.

It is said perception is reality. At least, it is the reality of the person owning the perception.

When First Georgia overcame its financial problems in 1976, I began preaching to our staff that we would eventually be a billion-dollar asset bank. That was my dream and perception. There was no real basis for this projection, other than my belief it could be accomplished if we stayed focused on our plans and worked like the devil to make it happen.

My dream was shared constantly with the officers and employees of the company for ten years. However, most people outside the immediate First Georgia family considered this prophecy to be ridiculous.

Dreams and visions have a unique way of becoming reality if a person wants something badly enough and believes it can happen. This assumes, of course, that they have done their homework, prepared properly, are 1000% committed, and work like hell to make them happen.

The more you talk about your vision, convert others to the same belief, and stay focused on your objective; you have a good chance of achieving your perceived goal.

We stayed the course, the vision was constantly vocalized to the staff, and we ultimately reached the "mountain top."

By the end of 1985 First Georgia Bank had assumed a new position among the financial leaders in Georgia. We were now the sixth largest commercial bank in the state and the 350th largest of approximately 14,000 banks in the United States.

First Georgia had also become the largest and fastest growing bank in the First Railroad & Banking Company system. This progress surprised many of our distracters in the banking community.

When 1986 began there were new challenges and opportunities beginning to unfold in the banking world and many of those would affect First Georgia's destiny.

The major financial institutions around the country were in the hunt to enlarge their franchises. They were beginning a major push to make multiple acquisitions in their quest for expansion and market share growth.

First Railroad and Banking Company was one of the early targets identified by industry analysts as a good acquisition prospect.

The company owned 12 banks in growing Georgia markets, an interest in a data processing company, First Financial Management, and had acquired a large finance subsidiary, CMC Financial, headquartered in Charlotte, North Carolina. The combined asset size of the company was $4 billion. The management team had received high marks in the investment community over the years for their solid performance.

Everything about First Railroad including the size, earnings, location, and the acquisition fervor of the market place seemed to indicate it would only be a matter of time before an interested purchaser knocked on the door.

Several of the presidents of the subsidiaries recognized the nature of the changing times, and accepted the likelihood that First Railroad would eventually be purchased by a stalking suitor in the near future. But, no one knew how soon or when the transaction would ultimately occur.

My intuitive feeling told me the senior management of the company, supported by the board of directors, were ready to call it quits, sell out, cash in their stock, and go on with another life. The timing was right and everyone seemed to have that look in their eyes. It was a feeling in my bones and the realization that all things finally come to an end, especially when money is the prime motivator.

So certain of the logical progression of future events by management, I wagered a small sum with one of the other company presidents betting that First Railroad would have a deal announced by July 1, 1986.

My projection was made during the early weeks of March at a corporate planning session. I won the bet by 15 days, with no insider information.

On June 15,1986 an announcement appeared in the business pages of the Atlanta Journal-Constitution newspaper with the details of the sale of First Railroad to the Charlotte, N.C. based First Union Corporation.

However, two days prior, on Friday, June 13, the newspaper announced my departure from First Georgia and acceptance of the position as the President and Chief Executive Officer of Georgia Federal, a Federal Savings Bank, in Atlanta.

The "tea leaves" had been read correctly concerning the sale of the company. My intuition also told me there would be no place for me in the acquiring organization.

I was confident a new owner would more than likely make significant management changes, which is normal with most acquisitions, and would want their own corporate executive running the Georgia organization from Atlanta. I would be the odd-man-out once the deal was completed, regardless of any past successes. Post acquisition events within First Railroad proved my analysis to be on target.

Fortunately, two months earlier, J. B. Fuqua, Chairman of Fuqua Industries Inc., an Atlanta based company and new owner of Georgia Federal Savings Bank, had approached me about my interest in joining the bank as president.

I had decided some months earlier, prior to the sale of First Railroad that it was time to move on, if a better career opportunity was presented. My timing and luck could not have been better.

Actually, after Fuqua had purchased Georgia Federal, I had confidentially considered the possibility of undertaking that position if it was presented. Knowing Fuqua's propensity to make changes in the organizations they purchased, and thinking they would hire a qualified banker to help facilitate a transition of the thrift into a bank-like organization, I was hopeful my name might be put into the "pot" for consideration.

It would be a great opportunity with significant growth possibilities. I did not share my thoughts with anyone, but I began to hear some "rumblings" that my name had been mentioned.

During May a call came to my office asking if I would meet with J.B. Fuqua. I responded positively.

After several weeks of discussion about financial terms, authority, responsibility, and the proposed new direction for the bank, I accepted Fugua's offer two days prior to the announcement of the sale of First Railroad.

However, one minor detail remained. Fuqua Industries had high expectations for their new acquisition, and it was obvious an abundance of organizational and infrastructure changes would be required to meet those expectations.

During the early discussions, while learning about the amount of transition that was expected to occur, I concluded it was important for the new president to also have the title of CEO. Otherwise, it would be difficult to meet the objectives on a defined schedule. I decided not to take the job without the title under any other scenario. Attempting to operate without absolute power would be a formula for failure in this situation.

John Zellars was the current Chairman and President. He had done a good job managing the company, as a thrift or savings bank, and he had an excellent reputation in the industry. John had held numerous positions in various trade organizations, while spending over thirty years of his life in the business.

However, his knowledge of commercial banking was limited, and I knew many structural changes would need to be made quickly within the company. I did not want to dwell on the operational necessity and legislate every decision over an extended period with anyone except the owner. However, I did believe Zellers would be cooperative in most cases. That trait was evident in his nature.

As the chief executive, it would be much easier to get on with the process without protracted discussions with the former head of the company, and move more rapidly toward the ultimate objective: Transforming Georgia Federal into a commercial bank type organization and facilitating the culture changes necessary to make it work.

After a period of extended discussions, Fuqua worked out an arrangement with Zellars, who was near retirement age, and he agreed to function as the Chairman and relinquish the other titles of Chief Executive Officer and President to me.

During the next three years John worked diligently to assist in his new role. It was a difficult situation for him, but he was rewarded properly for his cooperation and willingness to play a lesser, but important role in the new organization.

The largest personal difficulty in the decision to change employment, besides leaving the employees who had worked so hard to make First Georgia successful, was how to inform Carl Sanders about this new opportunity and my decision to leave the bank. After 12 years working with him, I didn't have a clue on how to break the news.

Mr. Fuqua, who was a personal friend and had many past business and political associations with Carl, told me he would talk with him about our discussions. Carl was also a member of the Fuqua Industries board.

Nevertheless, I still had concern, but Fuqua said, "Carl was a big boy and would understand."

He did, just as Fuqua predicted. A few days later Sanders called me and said, "Dam it Dick are you really going to leave me?" He then told me it was a great opportunity and not to turn it down, especially with the uncertainty about First Railroad and pending sale of the company. The purchase by First Union was announced shortly after our conversation.

Good managers are understanding when their employees have an opportunity to better themselves financially or professionally. Unless they can counter the proposal with

something of greater value or enhanced opportunity they will support the employee's decision in a positive manner. Life is just too short and memories too long for any leader to respond differently.

It is amazing how people's paths can cross in various situations during their lives. I have always believed it is best to treat your associates with honor and integrity, because you may just end up working for them at some point. It happened to me.

On July 1, 1986 my new career began in the Savings and Loan or S&L industry upon reporting to the headquarters of Georgia Federal, which was only four blocks from my First Georgia office.

There was an invaluable lesson to be learned from this transition. I believed building a solid, financially strong, and well performing organization would enable it to weather almost any adversity. I told my management team, prior to my departure, that their continued future with the company was assured, because of First Georgia's past performance and reputation in the Atlanta market---my assessment was very wrong and terribly naive.

In less than three months, after First Railroad was acquired, my former organization, First Georgia Bank, ceased to exist as I had known it.

After the acquisition, a new management team was quickly assimilated from the acquiring company, and most of my former executives were either relegated to lesser positions or given the opportunity to seek other jobs.

The marketing and advertising programs were eliminated and many of the bank's corporate customers were asked to find other banking relationships. Apparently, they did not fit the credit profile or standards of the new owners.

The corporate culture we had worked so hard to install over the previous years disappeared immediately. A new broom sweeps clean, aptly describes the actions most frequently taken post acquisition of a company.

This experience taught me just how fleeting all fame and success can be. Most organizations in their original form will not persist under radical change, regardless of the past efforts and time employed to create the so-called masterpiece.

It is best not to let your personal pride get in the way of your thinking and believe someone will bronze your chair for posterity when you are gone. It does not happen that way in a world where profit and loss are the key movers and shakers in the final equation.

Part of the process and enjoyment of buying anything is the satisfaction experienced by a new owner in making changes to fit their model, culture, and operating philosophy. Past performance is important up to the time a company is acquired, but the future will be measured against different standards established by the new owner and management team.

Indeed, the changes may not result in improvements in performance; nonetheless, the buyers have spent their money and earned the right to do as they deem appropriate with their new play toy.

Normally, after an acquisition the sellers with their pocketbooks greatly enhanced, slither away with their largess. They split the spoils with the happy shareholders and go on to other and now more important things.

Although saddened by the abrupt changes within First Georgia, I found solace when encountering members of our former staff, and they would tell me how much they had enjoyed working at the bank and how personally rewarding the experience had been.

A manager or leader can never achieve more in their career than the acknowledgement, from their former employees or troops, about the amount of pride and enjoyment they experienced, while a member of the organization.

Now, at Georgia Federal Bank I had more pressing things to dwell on. Learning the rudiments of the savings & loan business, changing the business orientation of the company, and living through and surviving the dramatic rehabilitation and restructuring of the entire thrift industry.

Although typically enjoying change and challenge in my life, these "new opportunities" would cover ground I had never plowed before. It was impossible to anticipate the difficulties and problems in this business and the gigantic proportions they would eventually grow to over the next few years.

A number of thrift industry specialists and institutional incumbents, with far greater knowledge and experience than me, had no idea that their world was about to be altered forever.

The Savings and Loan business was fast becoming a financial debacle, a scandal, and disaster. It would eventually impact our nation with losses of nearly **One Trillion Dollars**.

Chapter Nine
Georgia Federal Bank, FSB

The Georgia Federal Bank, FSB (Federal Savings Bank) headquarters building was located in the center of the city on Marietta Street at five points, immediately adjacent to the First National Bank Tower, my first employer in Atlanta.

Over a period of 20 years of banking in Atlanta, I had now moved only about 50 yards, which was the approximate distance from my original office in the First National tower to my new location at Georgia Federal. I always thought this was an interesting way to describe career advancement in the banking industry.

The bank was the largest savings and loan in Georgia and the 46th largest in the nation with $2.8 billion in assets and 65 branches located throughout the state.

Additionally, the bank had recently purchased a consumer finance company, First Family Financial Services Inc., from the First National Bank of Atlanta and was in the process of hiring a new president to run this highly profitable organization.

Georgia Federal had been converted from mutual ownership, which is depositor owned, to a publicly traded stock company in 1984.

Fuqua Industries had tendered for the stock of the company paying approximately $250 million and now had sole ownership effective April 1986. This purchase occurred just one month prior to the time J. B. Fuqua approached me with a job offer.

The new owners had decided the company needed some financial engineering done to the balance sheet to enhance its earnings potential. They had also concluded the operating systems needed a substantial upgrade in order to facilitate new product innovations, acquisition possibilities, and the resultant growth projections.

Fuqua envisioned the company looking and functioning like a commercial bank with similar banking type products and marketing programs. All of these planned initiatives were to be implemented in short order after the company was acquired.

It was also expected a new management team, with commercial banking experience, would be brought on board to install the necessary modifications and conversion of the institution to a commercial bank-type organization.

The Fuqua management believed Georgia Federal was a "sleeping giant," and the earnings of the company could be considerably improved with their plans and guidance. This was the principal reason for the purchase of the bank.

The hiring of a new president with a commercial banking background would to be the first step in Fuqua's plan to start the transformation of the company. They rationalized someone with banking experience, who possessed the ability and knowledge to get the job done effectively and quickly, was needed in that position.

I had been asked by one of my directors, William Suttles, Provost of Georgia State University, who was also a director at Georgia Federal, if I would be interested in talking with Mr. Fuqua about a position with the bank. I responded favorably.

As a result of eventually accepting Fuqua's offer at Georgia Federal, I would have a front row seat in the Thrift Theater over the next seven years watching and participating in the **S&L Hell,** as the author, Kathleen Day, described it in her book of the same name.

Some background on the history and problems of the Thrift or S&L industry might be useful in order to put the issues in the appropriate perspective.

Since the early 1900's the number of thrift institutions had declined from about 12,000 to around 5,000, and commercial banks had dwindled from a high of 30,000 to about 14,000 at the time of my entry in the banking scene in 1968.

A sizable number of financial institutions had failed after the stock market crash in 1929 and the Great Depression immediately following.

Also, as the economy began to recover from the crisis of the twenties and thirties, a large number of mergers were propagated within the financial industry, which also produced a reduction in the number of individual institutions.

After the nation stabilized and the economy finally recovered, the surviving companies took a more conservative approach with their lending practices and business plans.

By the late seventies, periods of inflation, interest rate deregulation, competition, poor management, risky loan generation, and just pure greed began to impact this industry sector.

The thrift segment seemed to take the greatest hit, and when interest rates peaked in 1982 at 18+%, many of these companies were beginning to slide into a deep hole of insolvency.

Re-regulation of the industry in the eighties, by the banking regulators and U. S. government, was initiated with the anticipation the problems could be mitigated, if the regulations were altered. They were changed and the problems worsened.

Thrifts were provided with greater freedom within their product lines, loan origination, and portfolio acquisitions, including the investment in high yield, high-risk, junk bonds.

The high interest rate environment of the early eighties, combined with more risk taking by many of these institutions with their new mandated powers of investment and lending, led to more troubled companies and eventual failures. As 1984 began, approximately 3500 thrifts were left in operation.

The already deep-seated issues continued to plague the industry, and by 1988 only 3,000 thrifts remained with their doors opened, many with loan and investment problems yet to be reckoned with.

By 1993, there were less than 2,000 thrifts in existence. Today, there are approximately 1100 thrifts remaining in the industry. However new thrift charters are now being issued on a controlled and limited scale today.

During these years of the industry decline and failures, Congress continued to promote new rules and regulations to help control and lessen the problems. Some worked and some did not, because many of the institutions were well beyond repair.

A few banks and other financially related companies purchased some of the troubled thrifts with the hope of expanding their business lines and market size. Many of the more high-risk insolvent thrifts were closed in perpetuity and their remaining good assets were sold to the highest bidder.

The losses from these transactions were ultimately absorbed by the taxpayer in the form of excess government expenses. Actually, these losses were nothing more than write-offs or write-downs of semi-worthless assets, which were owned by the institutions.

This was the financial climate existing in the industry when I joined Georgia Federal in the mid-summer of 1986. Although, the overall environment within the S&L industry was not good, there were some thrifts in the country still financially sound and performing satisfactorily in their markets. Georgia Federal was one of those institutions.

Transforming and changing the mindset and business approach of a company, or any organization for that matter, requires a major shift in its operating philosophy, management team, and culture. My new employer, Georgia Federal Bank, would require that same attention and effort.

Realizing this, I discussed my new challenge and opportunity with Tom Peters, while attending one of his seminars in California, a few months after joining the bank.

I was particularly interested in his views on the amount of time required to alter the culture of a company. Especially one that had operated in a relatively conservative industry and not been progressive or shown much in the way of new business dynamics.

His response was shocking. From his experience and consulting work he told me it would take at least five years to make the shift. It was my opinion I would be history by then, if it took that long.

He chuckled and told me to do some dramatic things quickly, if I wanted to expedite a cultural shift in attitude and performance, and to begin immediately. He told me not to worry about making mistakes, but to do the things necessary, and to let the employees know what was expected of them.

Peters made another interesting point. He said a manager on a job is basically **"bullet proof"** when they initially take on a new position with a company. He said, "they are normally given total freedom and are untouchable for a short period of time in their decision process."

"The boss," he said, "will normally let the new manager do whatever he or she believes necessary for about a six-month period, because they don't want to admit they made a hiring mistake. After that period of time the principals will begin to assert themselves more frequently, and the honeymoon will be over."

He reasoned it would be prudent to implement everything I wanted to do as quickly as possible, because the road of change would be much more difficult to travel later on.

Taking his recommendation to heart, I would soon discover he had been on target with his projection. My honeymoon, with my new bosses, lasted until the end of the first year, about six months!

Fortunately, I had some experience in trying different and crazy things and it didn't take long to put some schemes together to attack the cultural and general organizational issues.

My first initiative was the introduction of the Executive Adventure Program, which was the same outdoor training that had been successful in molding the culture at my former company.

An article, on the First Georgia program, had recently appeared in the Atlanta Journal-Constitution newspaper some weeks prior to me joining Georgia Federal.

It was a full-page story on our training process with a picture of one of our branch managers crawling across a rope suspended between two trees some fifty feet from the ground. It was titled, **"Execs get tough, find gung ho spirit at bankers' boot camp."**

When it was formally announced I would be the next CEO at Georgia Federal, many of the bank's employees, all of whom had seen the story, were upset and concerned about being required to participate in this kind of training. They would learn to adapt in short order.

The Atlanta based Georgia Trend magazine, also published another article a few months earlier with the headline **"Dick Jackson Uses the Rambo Approach to Running A Bank."**

It was a profile of my past banking experiences in Atlanta and the writer alluded to many of the outdoor programs we had completed at First Georgia and the "take no prisoners" approach to our sales culture. These stories were probably humorous to some of the employees at Georgia Federal, but one point was clear, they got their attention.

Over the next 12 months, 300 managers would go to the woods and experience the thrill of learning how to be an effective team member, assume greater risks, enhance camaraderie within their staffs, and build their personal self-confidence.

All of this would occur while they were swinging through the trees on ropes and climbing over wooden obstacles in the name of character building.

As was the standard approach, each group was debriefed at the end of the course, as to the lessons learned, followed by discussion on how they could use this newfound information to enable them to perform at a higher level in the organization. We regularly used every conceivable opportunity to work on their "hearts and minds" to affect the change in our culture.

During my earlier conversation with Tom Peters about culture change, we also discussed the possibility of continuing the same **In Search of Excellence "Skunk Works"** seminars that been conducted at First Georgia. He thought it would be a good idea.

Bob LeDuc, Tom's associate, who had administered the training at my former bank, was again given a similar task to conduct this phase of our training and was scheduled to start the instruction within a few months after I joined Georgia Federal.

Bob was to emphasize sales, customer service, value enhancement, leadership, and the methodology of getting things done quickly and efficiently. He was an excellent instructor and carried the messages superbly to our staff.

We had no time to waste, at least in my mind. Hopefully, everyone in the organization would soon share the same feeling.

During the seminars, when Bob was asked by some of the employees why he was conducting this particular training his standard response was; " I am here to explain Dick Jackson and the kind of performance he will be looking for from all of you."

After that answer, no other remarks were required concerning the propriety and necessity of the training.

It was interesting to experience the changes in our employees, after they were exposed to these training seminars.

Some would accept the concepts and ideas easily and gravitate immediately toward implementing them into their management routine.

Others would struggle and fight within themselves for understanding, because they found the ideas and concepts foreign to them and vastly different from anything they had been exposed to in the past.

Some minds were open to new ideas, some were not. We had to find those that could and would change and unfortunately weed-out those people, who could not make a work adjustment.

We actually had some employees come and tell us they did not think they could make alterations in their management style, or adopt the new principles we were attempting to inculcate into their demeanor. Rather than fail and embarrass themselves, they opted to resign on their own, and seek a work environment more suitable to their old methods.

Personally, I respected this honesty and offered to help them in any way possible. In most cases, their decisions were in the best interests of both the bank and their on-going career.

It took a lot of **"guts"** for them to step forward and volunteer their feelings and initiate summary action. Perhaps they learned more than they realized from the instruction.

Much of the first year was devoted to changing the company attitude to facilitate the bank's new objectives: **A cultural shift toward a dynamic corporate environment, replete with inspired employees, who were enthusiastic about performing at their best.**

Finally, after exposing many of our managers to the different programs and making a number of personnel changes, we began to slowly experience the job behavior and attitude needed to meet our expectations and improve the company's performance.

Because of this total commitment and our concentrated efforts we improved Tom Peter's projection significantly to effect the culture shift at Georgia Federal. However, it is important to realize that change is never really over or complete.

A philosopher once said, "When you're through changing, you're through."Continuous attention has to be given throughout the life of the company to the changing role of culture and it must be emphasized by management at every opportunity. It is essential for the executives to "walk the talk" to ensure the organization continues to mature and adapt to the ever changing needs and business opportunities of the company.

Savings and Loans or Thrift Institutions primarily focused their efforts in the home mortgage lending area, which was their mandate from the time the industry was first created. Georgia Federal, in 1986 was the most active lender in Atlanta in this particular market.

The bank's mortgage lending market share did decline over the next few years. The competition became greater from the commercial banks, when the regulations were changed, permitting them to aggressively engage in the mortgage market.

Georgia Federal was also active in the commercial real estate lending arena. Fortunately, the bank had made most of its loans in the state in close proximity to the branch network. This was contrary to the practice of many thrifts throughout the country at that time. Unfortunately, those institutions generated loans outside of their markets and were the most susceptible to losses, because of their inability to control the borrowers and effectively manage the lending process from a distance.

When the new regulations expanded the powers of thrift institutions, Georgia Federal began offering consumer checking accounts and had been very successful in marketing this product.

The bank accumulated a large base of these new accounts, about 75,000. This resulted in a high volume of checking transaction activity.

As a result of this growth and other product needs, the bank was nearly out of computer capacity. In addition, it did not have the operating capability to generate a flexible management reporting system.

It was necessary to immediately respond to this limitation. Consequently, we were soon immersed in a new IBM computer systems installation conversion costing over $7 million dollars.

Ultimately, our capital expenditures for the next three years would exceed $30 million for additional systems improvements, computer terminals, and branch office expansion. Unfortunately, very little had been done in the previous period to install state-of-the-art technology in the company.

The bank's qualified technical staff was augmented by representatives of our vendor suppliers and representatives from the various user departments to accommodate this technology change. Nonetheless, we had our share of technical difficulties surface during and after the work was completed.

Because of the failure to run a single computer conversion program during the final stage of installation, the bank's accounting ledgers were out of balance by several billion dollars at the conclusion of the project. This almost resulted in a "financial meltdown of the company," as one of our internal accountants described it, because the bank could not balance its books.

It took several months of precious time and effort to correct this costly error, resulting in a change of management within the data processing department during the clean-up period.

In the Marine Corps these mishaps, bad decisions, and lack of follow-up resulting in confusion were referred to as a **FUBAR. "Fucked Up Beyond Absolute Recognition."** Unfortunately, I experienced a lot of **"Fubars"** during my years in the Marines and the banking business, some probably caused from my own devices.

Regardless of the amount of planning and thought that goes into a systems conversion, it is mandatory for management to take nothing for granted during the project. Extensive and frequent checkpoints should be programmed, conducted on a timely bases and documented during each phase of the implementation.

A key reminder: There is always something else remaining to be done. If you don't keep this principle in mind in most things you do, your final efforts will probably be negatively impacted. It is far better to anticipate potential problems and that something will probably go wrong. Plan accordingly. It will save both time and money in the long run.

After an analysis of our marketing program we decided to hire a new advertising agency to create a fresh and more aggressive image for the bank.

Georgia Federal had a tag line it used in most of its material: **"The Can Do Bank."** We did not think it was a progressive theme and it had become somewhat "tired" in execution.

It was important for our advertising program to achieve a "top of mind" awareness in the market, regardless of the medium used. We wanted something that would make a strong statement in the media about the "new" Georgia Federal Bank.

We began interviewing candidates for the marketing director position and finally concluded that my former director, Judy Horton, who had been at First Georgia for several years, was the best suited and the most qualified for the position.

After some discussion, she agreed to leave the new owner, First Union, where her future was in doubt anyway and join Georgia Federal. With her on board we were now positioned to hire the agency and introduce a totally different adverting approach.

Judy had done a superior job at First Georgia, and according to a couple of personnel headhunters; she was one of the most qualified marketing professionals in the city. She would later become one of the few women Executive Vice Presidents in Atlanta.

We selected J. Walter Thompson as our new agency. They had a large office in Atlanta and seemed to be the most aggressive in the pursuit of our account.

Their Washington office handled the Marine Corps advertising program, which was probably a plus with me in the selection process.

First Georgia had been awarded several Addy advertising awards, and with Judy's guidance and the efforts of our new agency, Georgia Federal would repeat this feat with Gold Addys for film, video production, television, and local campaign awards over the next several years. We also won the International Mobius Award for television commercials at the United States Festivals Association. These were bright achievements, especially for an "old traditional savings and loan organization."

Our campaign theme was changed from "The Can Do Bank" to **"Real Life Banking,"** and later to **"Two Words To The Wise---Georgia Federal."** This specific "tag" line symbolized and addressed the type of people, who elected to bank with GFB, as being intelligent and financially aware of good banking opportunities and practices.

During the next seven years our assets grew by over $2 billion to $4.7 billion, without acquisitions. Most of our product line growth, on a percentage basis, equaled or exceeded that of our competition.

Bank-sponsored lunches and cocktail functions were conducted in cities where we had branch offices. One of our senior executives would speak at these events and provide updates on the industry, economy, and of course, the status of Georgia Federal.

We were able to obtain excellent coverage on these events in the local newspaper. In addition, we would also endeavor to "press the flesh" with most of our customers and banking prospects in these areas. Meeting people under any venue was one of the "master tenets" in our sales approach.

The programs were helpful with the growth of these local offices. But, most importantly they emphasized senior management's commitment to our smaller markets and willingness to support them totally in their business development efforts.

Unfortunately, in many organizations, the staff members located distantly from the headquarters do not receive the same level of attention as their counterparts. The management of Georgia Federal was committed to ensuring this did not occur.

We made certain through regularly scheduled visits, employee recognition events, and customer functions that our staff knew management appreciated their efforts, and they were important to the overall success of the company.

Management should never take their employees for granted or fail to give equal and frequent recognition for a job well done, or for that matter, the expectation it will be done. If practiced routinely, the final results will normally mirror those expectations.

Several years ago the Western Electric Company conducted a study at one of their plants on productivity.

New overhead lighting was installed in the workspaces of a select test group of production workers. Afterwards, the overall output improved substantially. The other test group, consisting of workers who did not have the improved lighting installed, remained at the same level of production.

When the emphasis on the lighting improvements were reversed for the two test groups, the results for the new group improved, while the initial test group declined to their former performance levels.

The people conducting the tests eventually concluded, after a number of different iterations that the lighting had nothing to do with improved production levels, but was a result of the personal attention given to the various groups of workers throughout the study.

These findings were ultimately called "The Hawthorne Effect." It cited a very basic principle of motivation.

The more positive attention your employees receive, the more their performance levels will likely improve.

The Marine Corps doctrine teaches its leaders that one of the most important ways a commander can influence the resulting outcome of combat is by his presence on the battlefield. This principal is of critical importance in war and business.

Always go where the action is. Your people will know you are readily available to support them if necessary. It is important for leaders to have the "smell of the battlefield" about them. They can then properly evaluate the situation and make changes consistent with the needs of the organization and the ever changing tactical or business conditions. Leaders can't do that from a rear position. They must place themselves where they can influence, guide, and if required, personally direct the activities or action.

Fuqua Industries Inc., the new owner of Georgia Federal, was a type of conglomerate organization owning a number of unrelated consumer product companies in unrelated industries.

The company holdings at the time the bank was purchased included Snapper Power Equipment, a manufacturer/wholesaler of rear-engine riding lawnmowers and self-propelled walk behind mowers. Colorcraft Industries, the nation's leading photo-finisher. American

Seating Corporation, the market leader in seating for buses, railcars and stadiums, and Fuqua Sports Equipment, a wholesaler of sporting, physical fitness, and camping gear.

Revenues were in excess of $800 million. Both the profits and stock price of Fuqua industries were growing steadily.

Many people, who had invested in the company stock over the years, had achieved a solid return on their investment. There were those who considered the Chairman and CEO, J. B. Fuqua, to be a financial wizard of sorts. The financial success and history of the company seemed to back-up those beliefs.

Fuqua had been in the business for years of buying companies, building the franchise and then selling them for a nice profit when the market conditions were right.

Although, this may not have been the original objective when the bank was purchased, Georgia Federal would eventually fit into the same transaction mold for Fuqua.

The company's success, to a large extent, resulted from the ability to identify companies with good products, buy them at a favorable price, and then hire top-notch management talent to run the various entities. The "hired guns" were paid well, given sizable stock option opportunities, and held strictly accountable for their organizational performance. It was a good formula and it worked.

However, when a manager or a company failed to perform according to expectations, they were dispatched rapidly to the "happy hunting grounds."

Failure was not tolerated for any extended period and every person, who joined the Fuqua organization, knew the rules of the game.

Working under the demands of J. B. Fuqua and his talented President, Larry Klamon, who was a former corporate attorney, along with the other financial whiz kids in the headquarters, was not an easy task.

Detailed strategic and financial planning was a must. After a couple of early failed attempts presenting the bank's business plans, which were criticized appropriately for lack of supporting data, I rapidly learned how to conduct better research, organize, and present the bank's plans in a more acceptable manner to the Fuqua management team.

It was a hard lesson in humility, and it was necessary to learn quickly from those mistakes, otherwise, I would have ultimately visited those "happy hunting grounds."

It was discipline like this, which made Fuqua Industries successful and admired in the investment and business world.

Fuqua had successfully issued high-yield, Junk Bonds in its early corporate life and believed these were good instruments for financing a business. The company bonds had a high rating, had always been paid on time, and the company was obviously considered to be a very good credit risk.

The regulations had recently changed in the S&L industry and now allowed thrifts to purchase these types of debt instruments for their investment portfolio.

The Fuqua organization determined Junk Bonds would financially enable Georgia Federal's earnings. Subsequently, a procurement process was established to enable the bank to take advantage of this high-yield investment opportunity.

Junk Bonds were debt instruments with a high interest rate attached resulting from the credit rating of the issuing company. The higher rate paid on the bonds occurred due to the nature of the business or financial weakness of the company. The maturity of the bonds could range from 5 to 20 years.

Because of the higher yields, ranging from 8% to 18%, depending on the credit rating of the issuing company, the regulators assumed the acquisition of this product would help many of the struggling institutions substantially improve their profitability. Thrifts were allowed to invest up to 11% of their assets in Junk Bonds.

These bonds were not a means to an end, but the yields were much higher than could be earned in mortgage lending and in other investment opportunities. The credit risk associated with these debt instruments was also much higher, a factor some managers had downplayed in their pursuit to improve the profitability of their institution.

Many thrifts jumped into the junk bond market with great enthusiasm and bought bonds rapidly from any investment firm peddling them. The bad news about this product would come later when some of the issuing corporate entities could no longer service their debt.

However, this was not a consideration at the time, and the investment companies made a "killing" selling these new investment products to the uninitiated and unsuspecting thrifts.

The prospect of entering this market was frightening, because I had no experience in the investment or management of these debt instruments.

Commercial banks were not permitted to own these bonds; although, they could invest in government bonds and tax-free municipals, which were more familiar, less risky, and consequently highly acceptable to me. Besides, the name Junk Bond did not seem to portend a quality type investment.

I made every effort to postpone the decision. Initially, our investment department purchased a large number of municipals with a respectable tax equivalent yield of 8%. We anticipated this tactic might serve the purpose of satisfying our owner's thirst for improved profitability. It did not.

Soon afterwards, I found myself visiting several investment houses including Merrill Lynch, First Boston, and the Junk Bond kingmaker, Michael Milken of Drexel Burnham Lambert, at his office in Beverly Hills, California. Milken was the father of the Junk Bond investment vehicle and was instrumental in making this type of financing a fad within the business community.

The more time spent researching and talking with the so-called experts in the field, the more concerned I became.

Nevertheless, we proceeded as instructed, finally contracting with the First Boston investment group to provide their services and management expertise in building our portfolio.

Using the regulatory guideline of 11% of assets, Georgia Federal could purchase $300 million of these bonds for the investment portfolio. However, time ran out and the bank was sold before we reached that lofty number.

Georgia Federal did build a portfolio of approximately $150 million, over the following 12 months, with an average annual yield of 12%. The yield was terrific; the risk assumption, in my estimation, was horrible.

When the bank was sold to First Financial Management Corporation in 1989, the bonds were disposed of prior to the consummation of the sale. The bank experienced a loss of about $3 million on the entire portfolio. Our timing was perfect, because two weeks after the bonds were sold, the market crashed.

However, the bank had achieved a good investment return on the portfolio prior to the sale of the company. We also had established ample loss reserves from our earnings to more than cover any deficiency, and not affect the safety and soundness of the bank.

We were fortunate to have made the decision to sell the bonds when we did. If we had waited another 15 days, our losses would have been substantially higher, over $12 million dollars.

There is an old and very appropriate maxim that runs:

"It's better to be lucky than good."

Chapter Ten
Endgame

One of the best assets owned by Georgia Federal was its subsidary, First Family Financial Services Inc. It was a consumer finance company, managed by an experienced and capable executive, Alan Chalmers.

Chalmers was hired a few weeks after I joined the company when the former president, Ed Forsberg, retired.

J. B. Fuqua had served on the bank board, after making a large personal investment of several million dollars in the bank, when it converted from a mutual organization and went public.

Approximately two years later, his company, Fuqua Industries, ultimately tendered and purchased all the stock of the company.

He recommended to the board and management that Georgia Federal purchase First Family from the First National Bank of Atlanta when it was put up for sale.

It was probably the best decision made at the bank up to that time. First Family generated consumer loans with a gross yield in excess of 21%, and ultimately contributed nearly half of the earnings of the Georgia Federal operation.

First Family had an excellent franchise. They were located primarily in the southeast with assets of approximately $200 million when purchased.

As time progressed, it was determined that Georgia Federal could improve its earnings faster by growing First Family than by investing in other bankable assets. We elected to funnel many of our investment dollars into this subsidiary, by purchasing other small loan companies and merging them into the First Family organization, instead of totally focusing on the bank's growth.

This strategy paid enormous dividends. First Family grew to nearly $500 million in total assets by 1993.

It was eventually sold to First Associates for approximately $225 million that same year. Al Chalmers continued to run the company after the sale and retired in 1999.

An interesting aside to this successful operation occurred when the the Office of Thrift Regulation and Safety (OTS), located in Atlanta and responsible for the regulation of the industry in this district, informed us that First Family had grown so rapidly it was now considered a problem to the bank's safety and soundness.

They reasoned it was generating too many consumer loans as a percentage of the Georgia Federal's total assets. The OTS assumed this concentration of loans could eventually create a risky credit situation for the bank, if declining economic conditions were to impact this consumer segment.

Furthermore, the bank now had what the OTS considered to be too many high-rate consumer loans in its portfolio. They believed the loans were not of the best quality, because of their nature, generally oriented to people with lower incomes or with a low credit standing, and this could result in excessive credit losses in a problem economy.

The OTS wanted the bank to divest its ownership of the company as soon as practical even though first Family had never in its history suffered any large losses. The finance company had always been profitable and operated with very good credit underwriting procedures.

I was stunned by the request. First Family was one of our best earning assets and had performed in an excellent manner during the time of our ownership.

Additionally, it had contributed significantly to the growth of our capital with their ever-expanding profits. Without First Family as a part of our operations, Georgia Federal's good financial performance would have been impacted unfavorably.

First Family was ultimately sold a few months later, in early 1993, just prior to the sale of the bank to First Union Corporation.

Acquiring assets and building a larger franchise takes time and can be very frustrating. We made several offers to purchase other thrifts in Georgia that were in financial difficulty, but could not finalize the deals because of social issues or management's inability to act on the deal. Theirs not ours.

Management of these companies summarily dismissed our offers for reasons that made no sense to me. Some of these thrifts had no place to go except out of business and eventually they did just that.

In some cases they were waiting for a "white knight" with plenty of money to rescue them or inject capital, which they hoped would breathe fresh air into their troubled institution. Some even believed they should be paid more than they were worth.

Eventually, these institutions were closed and the assets with value were sold by the regulators to the highest bidder. Georgia Federal purchased a $100 million portfolio of equity loans from Atlanta based Fulton Federal, the third largest thrift in the state, after they experienced financial difficulties and was eventually closed.

We had attempted to purchase that company and failed for reasons noted. It went out of business in 1991. We could have probably salvaged some of these companies, integrated them into our operation, and leveraged the resultant organization into a highly profitable concern. Perhaps, even creating some value instead of losses for the shareholders of those savings banks.

So much for what could have been. Some of these managers should have been "put away" to regain their mental health for their lack of insight and stockholder concerns.

The screening, evaluating, and hiring of a management team is more of an evolutionary process than revolutionary. I spent nearly three years putting the right people in place at the bank.

Upon joining Georgia Federal it was apparent some of the current management team would need to be changed if we were going to alter the direction and culture of the company. This was one of the principal reasons I wanted the title of CEO when I came on board.

It would not have been prudent to battle John Zellars, the current CEO, over any of the changes, including the possible protection of any "sacred cows" in the organization.

Incidentally, I thought this would make his life easier. New management would likely release some of the people he had hired; consequently, this arrangement would not put him in an unfavorable light in those relationships.

All of the executives in the company were quality people, but they did not have the experience or knowledge to direct Georgia Federal in the proposed new environment.

Don B. Stout, the executive vice president of Georgia Federal with over 20 years experience in the industry, had been with the company a few years and had functioned under John as the manager for all real estate activities of the company.

He was very knowledgeable, had a solid management reputation, was open-minded to new approaches, and the proposed direction for the company. I liked his attitude, energy, and his willingness to move forward with the new business and organizational initiatives.

Consequently, Don would be the only member of the previous management team to remain with the bank until it was ultimately sold to First Union.

An early decision was made to bring a legal staff in-house to facilitate our loan closing operation in the residential and commercial real estate lending areas.

We thought this change would be economical in the long run, allowing us to compete more aggressively and competitively by controlling the closing process when loans were made to our customers.

Hal Clark Jr., a talented attorney, was hired from the law firm, Gambrell, Clark, Anderson, & Stolz as a senior vice president to manage this operation and to serve as the general counsel for the bank.

He had worked with the industry for a number of years and had been involved with Georgia Federal when it was converted from a mutual savings institution to stock ownership in 1984.

Frank M. Malone Jr., a seasoned personnel director, was hired as the senior vice president of human resources. He had previously worked in personnel administration for Sears, Roebuck, & Company for 28 years.

Several senior executives were hired from my previous organization, First Georgia Bank, over a period of time, including Judy Horton, who managed our marketing division.

Terry Miller, also a senior vice president, who was in charge of corporate lending at First Georgia was hired to manage a similar start-up department at Georgia Federal.

This was a product line in the industry authorized by the new regulations and we intended to take advantage of the opportunity to offer this service.

Lending to small and medium size businesses had been the catalyst for the growth of First Georgia, and we hoped to emulate that success at Georgia Federal.

Ralph King, also an executive at my former bank, was brought into the organization as a senior vice president to establish and manage a new credit administration department for all bank-lending operations. The bank did have this important function in its organization structure, which was not uncommon for thrifts at the time.

Prior to joining First Georgia as the credit administrator, Ralph had worked for several years at First National Bank of Atlanta as a corporate National Division lending officer. He was one of the officers of that department I had traveled with when we initially introduced our cash management product 15 years earlier.

We also hired an excellent manager for our operations division. Art Sammons joined the company after we experienced the debacle of the computer systems conversion. With his extensive banking background and experience he was able to introduce a professional discipline into that department.

Alan K. Chalmers, who had been hired as the president of our subsidiary, First Family Financial Services, Inc. was also a member of Georgia Federal's management team.

Jim Box, who had served as the chief financial officer of First Georgia, was also hired to work in the financial department and function as the assistant CFO of the company.

Box would later become the CEO and President of ebank Financial Services, Inc., a Unitary Thrift Holding Company, the owner of ebank, a thrift institution located in Atlanta.

The most difficult position to fill was that of the chief financial officer. The owner, Fuqua Industries, wanted the most qualified person available. Preferably, someone who had good technical financial skills and experience in both the commercial banking and investment banking industries.

It was a good idea. But the difficulty was finding a highly qualified professional with those varied skills, who would be willing to join a thrift institution with all the publicized problems now beginning to plague the industry.

Another issue of importance involved the amount of money and benefits required in hiring a person of this caliber. The compensation package would obviously be well above the norm of our other management positions, resulting in a large salary difference with those executives.

This can be a problem in a structured company and can result in severe morale concerns among the other senior managers, unless the individual is a "super" performer, conscious of the various attitudes, and very careful with the situation.

After extensive discussions with numerous candidates, by both Fuqua and Georgia Federal, we finally found a qualified individual among the horde of people we interviewed.

He had been located by an executive headhunter, Patrick Pittard, manager of the local Hedrick and Struggles personnel firm. He had the necessary qualifications, but more importantly he was interested in the position.

We hired Charles Miller, who had been employed with a large commercial bank in Texas. He worked for Georgia Federal until it was purchased by First Financial Management three years later.

At that time we had to repeat the employment process for a new CFO, because our new owners had some specific requirements of their own and wanted to have input in deciding who should fill this important position.

The comfort level for both Fuqua Industries and First Financial, as both were heavily oriented toward sophisticated financial reporting, was of critical significance. The personal chemistry and professional respect had to be especially good between the subsidiary and corporate headquarters to ensure a positive working arrangement. This is not uncommon in business.

At the time we were purchased by FFMC, the chief financial officer of that company was Doug Schachner, who had only recently joined FFMC. He was a known quantity.

In a previous life he had been the CFO of First Railroad and Banking Company of Georgia. Pat Thomas and I had worked with Doug extensively, while managing our subsidiaries for that organization. Doug was a great person and probably one of the most knowledgeable financial executives in the banking industry.

He recommended we interview a young man, who had worked for him at his most recent employer in Charlotte. Discretion being the better part of valor, and highly desirous to maintain peace with our new family, we quickly responded favorably to his suggestion.

We fortunately found a "diamond in the rough" and hired Ray Emmons for the position. He became an outstanding chief financial officer for Georgia Federal, and most importantly, he had the confidence and support of our parent in all financially related matters. He subsequently filled a key financial position at First Financial for several years after the bank was sold.

This made my job much easier, and facilitated our recommendations for both capital projects and the financial engineering tactics we later employed with our balance sheet to improve interest rate risk and future earnings.

An important lesson learned that should be practiced frequently is the art of compromise. This is especially important if you're going to lose the battle anyway by resisting. It is far better "to bend than break" and live to fight another day. You will lose some battles, but in the end---win the war.

Another significant personnel addition to the company was William D. Farr. Bill had worked for the First National Bank of Atlanta for over 20 years and was an Executive Vice President of that organization.

It was determined a chief operating officer should be added to our company when we were purchased by FFMC. We were growing rapidly and there was no person designated in the organization to assume command if something happened to me.

We thought Bill would be an excellent addition and the perfect choice for the position. I had known him during my years at First National, as had Pat Thomas, and we had a good rapport with him personally. He was a knowledgeable and talented banker, who had an excellent banking reputation and was respected professionally by all those who knew him.

When we spoke about the position he was told this was a great opportunity and we thought he could maximize his banking experience and potential in this position. He finally agreed and we had our new chief operating officer on board in short order.

Bill was an excellent team player and made significant contributions to the company until it was sold to First Union Corporation. Afterwards, he undertook other part-time corporate ventures and board memberships in Atlanta.

All of these executives were loyal to the company and worked together well as a team. Without this committed group of managers, Georgia Federal would not have experienced the successful growth and earnings it achieved from 1986 to 1993.

Any new group of people, when initially brought together to run a company, or any organization for that matter, will experience adjustment problems and some infighting as a result of turf issues. It is essential for the senior executive to quickly and impartially deal with these issues in a fair and equitable manner to minimize the problem.

Conflict should be respected and in some cases encouraged to promote the best possible decisions. However, it must also be dealt with professionally and resolved honestly. Equality and fair treatment is essential and backstabbing cannot be tolerated if mutual respect is to be maintained.

There is always a challenge to maintain cohesiveness and cooperation within any group of responsible, personally driven, and high-energy people. For a manager to constantly achieve this balance within their organization they must be able to almost "walk on water."

Of course, any manager can do that, if they know where the rocks are hidden.---So to speak.

Reflection and review on progress or failures should be conducted on a regular basis by management after they have initiated their programs. Follow-through and monitoring of action plans is critical and must be a priority if the objectives are to be achieved. This facet of management is overlooked too many times.

After nearly three years of dedication and effort in bringing about a change in direction with Georgia Federal, it was apparent that progress had been made, albeit, it had come with pain and staff turnover.

It was emphasized in athletics and the Marine Corps that pain can and must be tolerated, as long as the results are positive and the struggle reaps the desired benefits. Also, any worthy effort will result in some number of casualties. These limitations, although never fully acceptable, are the price that is extracted when risks are taken to achieve the desired goal.

The most important objectives attained annually at Georgia Federal were profit and asset growth.

Throughout these years the company, even with problems in the economy and industry, had established new highs in growth, revenues, and net income. When all is said and done, these are the ultimate standards of measurement denoting success in most corporations.

The programs initiated by our management team were not revolutionary in nature, but they were aggressive and critical to the accomplishment of our objectives.

As I review them in 2003, some 10 years later with more knowledge about the business world, it is apparent that our business strategy and tactics at that time were sound, creative, and timely.

Perhaps, some of those plans could possibly be more significant in today's highly scrutinized business environment than they were in the eighties and nineties. Ours follow:

1) To be a sales and customer driven company. Absolute buy-in by the entire staff was essential.

2) To become highly competitive in our markets by offering more product opportunities, combined with an aggressive sales mentality.

3) To achieve excellence in all of our endeavors including sales, customer service, general business transactions, and employee training.

4) To establish high performance goals and gain commitment from all the staff members to reach these objectives.

5) To improve our branch system locations and make them more user-friendly for our customers.

6) To implement sales and production incentive programs to facilitate recognition and reward for those employees, who make superior contributions to the company.

7) To create a youthful, aggressive, and creative image for the bank with our advertising, public relations and marketing programs.

8) To create an environment which promotes fun and excitement in our work place for both our customers and employees.

9) To be a low-cost producer by fostering a bank-wide expense control culture.

10) Finally, to be a good corporate citizen in our community and emphasize integrity in all of our relationships within and outside our institution.

Although we were required to make many mid-course adjustments over the years, due to the ever-changing economic and volatile thrift industry environments, we never deviated from these basic objectives.

Just as a football halfback runs for the goal line, maneuvers around would-be tacklers, reverses his field, slows his step, then picks-up speed and hurdles the opposing tacklers as he runs his course, we made the same kind of effort with our company. And as the running back does, we always kept our eyes on the goal line.

Everything seemed to be going in the right direction for the bank. Profits were good, assets were growing, and the bank was performing extremely well, while the debacle of the thrift industry crisis continued to fester.

Suddenly, without any warning whatsoever, I was called to the Fuqua Industries headquarters for a discussion on a subject that had not been considered as even a remote possibility.

Without any fanfare, J. B. Fuqua and Larry Klamon informed me they had made the decision to sell Georgia Federal as soon as possible.

I was stunned upon hearing this, but not entirely disappointed, because I had experienced some difficult times with the Fuqua management style. However, it would only be fair to say that it was probably as much my problem as it was the parent's organization.

Georgia Federal had contributed significantly to the profits of Fuqua Industries; earning approximately 100 basis points on assets (ROA) during that time, which was an outstanding achievement for a thrift institution in the eighties. We had a relatively solid loan portfolio and the Fuqua stock price had risen during the time of bank ownership.

The formal announcement for the sale of the company was made in late 1987, only 18 months after Georgia Federal had been purchased. The reasons for the decision to sell were both strategic and financial in nature.

First, the bank did not fit the typical consumer market positioning of the other subsidiaries within the Fuqua organization, and they were considering the option of expanding more of their assets into those types of business lines.

Secondly, accounting changes were under consideration that would require corporations to include all assets and liabilities of their subsidiaries on the consolidated corporate balance sheet.

Due to the nature of a financial institution's statement of condition, the inclusion of bank loans and deposits on the consolidated financial statement would materially impact the calculation of the financial ratios and other related information. This would be confusing to both the current and future stockholders of the company.

Fuqua was asking in excess of $350 million for the company in a cash deal. The stock market at the time was not good, and with the troubles plaguing the thrift industry creating depressed values, both the timing and price for the sale of the company would ultimately be impacted.

Although, not unhappy about the prospects of the sale of the company, there was no way to forecast what future events and a new owner might hold in store for the company.

It had been a tough job managing a Federal Savings Bank in an industry on the brink of failure. This coupled with certain management disagreements had made my job very difficult. I hoped any change at this juncture would eventually be positive for both the company and me.

As a thrift institution we lived in a world of "guilt by association." We were continuously questioned by analysts as to our viability and capability for survival. It was an up-hill battle most of the time, even when we posted positive earnings figures. It seemed as if the investment brokers were always waiting for the "other shoe to drop."

The Fuqua management team and I had our share of disagreements during my tenure at the bank. Many of these were caused by the difficulty in running a company in the current troubled environment, while others evolved around differences in general operating philosophy and their "hands-on" involvement in the companies they owned. A few of these, unfortunately, received some amount of notoriety in the local newspapers.

Obviously, Fuqua Industries owned the bank and had every right to express ideas and provide direction for the bank's operations and performance.

Unfortunately, my reputation and operating style did not track that of a "good company man." Perhaps, I was a bit too gung-ho and self-reliant from my training in the Marine Corps to fit "snugly" into a highly controlled and centralized corporate management structure.

Probably, for my own good, too much responsibility and management freedom had been given to me in some past assignments in both the Marines and at First Georgia. This flexibility and leeway to operate with minimum supervision and oversight was difficult to overcome.

The challenge and invigoration of making my own decisions and being able to operate at the "edge of the envelope" without solicitation and interference from any corporate hierarchy greatly appealed to me. Meaning, being somewhat-out-of-bounds on rules and regulations was both personally exciting and highly stimulating.

While in Vietnam my unit was given a mission and total freedom to operate within our zone of action. We received little supervision and direction from our commander.

I had total control of my organization, and was much on my own as the leader most of the time. The same climate existed at my previous job. I never fully recovered from those liberties.

The corporate world entered at Georgia Federal was considerably different and the owners at Fuqua had their own management style, resulting from the many years of proven, highly successful operations.

The company mirrored Mr. Fuqua's personality and philosophy to some degree, and the resultant organization was very demanding and precise in its approach to business issues.

There was some friction and differences in how the bank should be operated and managed. Some adjustments were required to be made. Obviously, as the hired "gun slinger," I was the one designated to make the adjustments and finally did, although some of the changes were personally very painful.

At the conclusion of the relationship, when the bank was sold, it was apparent to me, even though the years under the Fuqua reign had been demanding; my learning curve had gone off the chart.

The ordeal provided me with a wider band of knowledge about the financial arena than I would have acquired in any other situation. The mental price paid for that experience was far greater than expected, but the educational return on my personal investment was beyond calculation.

Similar management issues would plague me with my next employer after the bank was purchased, and it is now painfully obvious that most of my education was from **"LESSONS LEARNED THE HARD WAY."** Eventually, the message became apparent, after finally realizing it was time to fit into the mold---or else.

Tough, talented, and ego-centered managers demand the best from their people and will typically imprint their own leadership style in an organization. That is their prerogative and the reason they occupy the position as the leader. Their subordinates need to understand and appreciate this uniqueness, personal drive, and strength. These are the characteristics of people who are capable of achieving superior goals that lesser inclined managers may fall short of obtaining.

Unquestionably, these were the kind of leaders I worked for during my business career. They were frustrating and difficult to please at times. But if you survived the relationship you came away with a positive appreciation of what you had learned under their guidance.

Recently, while reminiscing with Carl Sanders I humorously told him that a medal of some kind should be awarded to me for surviving the years under his leadership, and those of J.B. Fugua and Pat Thomas.

Carl was surprised at my comment and quickly came to his own defense by saying that he did not think he had personally been that difficult to work for. A moment later, after giving it more thought, he smiled and then added; "You're probably right."

These men were taskmasters and people of great accomplishment, who knew how to extract the best, and if desired, the worst from their executives. They probably got some of both from me.

The bank remained for sale for over 12 months, before a buyer with a rational business strategy emerged on the scene. And destiny had to play a role.

Several financial organizations had made overtures to purchase the company. However, most of them were "bottom feeders" or bargain hunters, who were attempting to purchase Georgia Federal below its value.

Early in the process, several well-known bankers around the country called Mr. Fuqua, inquired about the company, and over the telephone indicate a preliminary purchase price they would consider paying for the bank. In most cases it was well below the asking price

Mr. Fuqua, in his own classic unapproachable style, listened to their low-ball offers and then told them, in no uncertain terms, not to get on their airplane and fly to Atlanta, because he had no further interest in talking with them.

His tenacity and willingness to stick to his plan was worthy of note. However, time was beginning to run out for everyone. Fuqua wanted to dispose of the bank in order to proceed with other initiatives, and the management at Georgia Federal was having a difficult time maintaining morale and keeping people motivated about their jobs.

It would only be a matter of time before we began experiencing problems with both our staff and our customers, if we continued in this uncertain posture. It was damned tough to run a business when everyone in the country knew that it was for sale.

Our competition was sniping away at our customers and key employees. Rumors were flying about management and personnel changes. The continuing thrift industry malaise impacted the perception of our financial stability, and the employees were terrified that on any given day they would be without a job.

It was not a happy time for anyone. We were all running out of ideas on how to keep the organization functioning properly and our staff willing to continue with the bank during the uncertain times. We needed a plan, a change that would break the stalemate and breathe new life, opportunity, and viability into the bank.

The funny thing about life is that if you keep working, trying new approaches, don't give up, and keep hustling, while generally busting your ass, eventually, you may just arrive at the place that you need to be.

It always happens at the most inopportune time, frequently when you think the game is about over. Suddenly, without any warning, fate or providence stirs the inner source of your being, causing you to act differently or to choose another direction.

Perhaps, it's intuition or the left brain, your creative self, directing and carrying you without any realization on your part of the consequences. Or maybe it's destiny disguised in one of its many different forms.

For this particular situation destiny chose a bicycle ride on a Sunday afternoon. It unexpectedly carried me that day to an interested and substantially prominent Atlanta businessman, Patrick Thomas, the CEO of First Financial Management, Corporation. He was also an old friend from my early days at the First National Bank of Atlanta.

Pat had been involved and helpful with my employment at First Georgia Bank in 1974. In addition, my former bank had also used the computer services provided by his company for a number of years.

Frequently, on the weekends, I would take a long jog or bicycle ride to quiet my nerves and provide some quality time to gather my wits about the bank situation. Actually, these exercise periods not only cleared my mind and reduced the stress level, but often new ideas about the bank would creep-out of my nearly shattered brain, after all the mental clutter was jettisoned.

On this particular Sunday, while aimlessly peddling through the Sandy Springs area in North Atlanta for several hours, I decided to stop at Pat's home and have a chat and beg a beer.

The conversation immediately centered on the progress of the bank sale. I told him it was going very slow and the uncertainty was driving me crazy. The status was reviewed in some detail, and I opined it might go on for another year before an interested purchaser might emerge on the scene.

He listened carefully, as he was known to do on any business transaction. After my discussion he subtly mentioned he might be interested in purchasing Georgia Federal.

Frankly, his comment surprised me and I asked him why he would he want to buy a thrift institution with all the troubles and bad publicity existing in the industry?

My reasoning told me a commercial bank would be easier to acquire and less questionable, if he actually needed the services of a financial institution in his organization.

We met and talked a few more times, while biking through his neighborhood on subsequent weekends. After considerably more detailed conversation on the bank during these visits, he asked me to set up a meeting with the Fuqua people to discuss a potential deal.

Surely he was putting me on and I asked if his comment was made in jest. "No," he told me, " I am dead serious." He then explained why he was interested in buying Georgia Federal.

His company, First Financial Management, which was now a totally public company, was involved in the credit card processing business. This included the authorization, clearing, processing, and depositing of funds for all credit card transactions for his clients.

The competition for this highly lucrative business was gaining intensity. The major credit card issuers, such as Master Card, VISA, and American Express were attempting to prohibit third party processors, like FFMC, from processing their cards and using the payment system operated by the Federal Reserve Bank.

FFMC was in the process of purchasing several merchant credit card portfolios around the country. When those deals were completed, they would be the largest third-party provider of credit card authorizations and processing in the nation.

To ensure that the company was not restricted from participating in the growing credit card industry, Thomas had determined they would ultimately need to have uninhibited direct access to the payment system to maintain their competitive position.

Owning a financial institution would provide this assurance and the opportunity to develop additional financial relationships with their various customers.

This situation had been under study in his company for some time, and FFMC had actually looked at a couple of possible candidates to fill this role.

For one reason or another none of them seemed like the right fit. Some of the institutions had problems that could potentially redirect management's attention away from their mainline information processing business. Others had suspect management teams.

Georgia Federal appealed to Pat for several very important reasons. It was a local institution, based in Atlanta along with FFMC, and the bank's management was a known quantity. The asset size was appealing, because it offered synergies for both companies that were of a cost reduction and profit improvement nature.

The earnings of the bank had been good throughout the past several years. The American Banker newspaper ranked Georgia Federal as the 43rd top earner among thrifts in the country in 1988.

The bank was well capitalized, located in growing markets within Georgia, the loan portfolio was in relatively good condition, and all the lending business of the bank was focused in the State. Only First Family, the subsidiary consumer finance company, had offices outside of Georgia. Their performance had also been good during the time it was owned by the bank.

Finally, the continued deterioration of the thrift industry, resulting in depressed values of those institutions, along with Fuqua's stated interest in selling as quickly as possible, made the prospective negotiations favorable to FFMC.

Within a few days a meeting was arranged between FFMC and Fuqua Industries. With this discussion arranged, a glimmer of light was beginning to materialize at the end of the long and bleak tunnel we had been stuck in for the past year.

Conversation between the parties and due diligence by FFMC took several months of hard work and patience. As in any transaction of this kind, it nearly cratered several times. But, at the last minute, positive negotiations would again prevail and the prospective deal would be put back on track.

The most important points surrounding the transaction was Fuqua's enthusiasm and financial requirement to sell, and FFMC's operating need and specific interest to buy. The rest was mostly posturing by both parties to carve-out the best possible deal.

Larry Klamon, the president of Fuqua, knowing of my relationship with Thomas, asked me to work within the seams of the transaction, to help make it a workable deal for both parties. I practically ended-up representing the buyer and seller in the deal.

There were issues on both sides requiring attention. One of the most critical for FFMC was the $150 million Junk Bond portfolio in the bank.

After considerable discussion with both parties, we disposed of the entire portfolio before the transaction closed, and increased the general loan loss reserves of the bank. Both were major requirements in the purchase contract, and when completed, removed key irritants in the transaction for FFMC. Obviously, the other issue was price. After much conversation and negotiation a deal was finally arranged.

In June 1989, Georgia Federal was sold by Fuqua Industries for $235 million and became a subsidiary of First Financial Management Corporation.

On that day I sent my new boss and now owner of Georgia Federal, Pat Thomas, who like myself had spent several years in the military, an army helmet, a flak jacket, K-bar knife, and a box of C-rations with the following note: "Welcome to the S&L business, you may need these." He had a good sense of humor.

There was an interesting twist to this transaction, which occurred just before the deal was concluded.

At some period during the negotiations with FFMC, J.B. Fuqua had decided to sell his interest in Fuqua Industries to Charles "Red" Scott, President of Intermark, Inc.

This became public information. However, Scott asked Fuqua not to sell the bank before he bought the company, as he saw it as a stable income-producing asset in the Fuqua organization. It was not too late to stop the transaction with FFMC, because all the documents had not been finalized.

Scott's plan was to merge Fuqua into the InterMark Corporation, a company he personally had a large ownership position in. It would be the ultimate owner of Fuqua Industries.

A Company meeting, which included the executives from both organizations, was scheduled in Hawaii one month prior to the sale of the bank to FFMC.

At that meeting, Scott openly pleaded his position and desire about retaining control of the bank to the entire group of managers and staff. He literally harangued Larry Klamon, who was currently the President of Fuqua and would remain in that position after Scott acquired Fuqua, not to go through with the sale of the bank.

I was somewhat embarrassed about the matter and didn't understand why I had been invited to attend the meeting, since the sale of Georgia Federal was pending and was scheduled to close within a few weeks.

His obvious game plan was to use all possible means to retain ownership of Georgia Federal. I assume he thought he could use these methods and tactics to persuade Fuqua to rescind the bank sale at the last minute.

All of Scott's pleadings and efforts were wasted, falling on deaf ears. The deal with FFMC was concluded shortly thereafter, much to Scott's chagrin and Fuqua's obvious satisfaction.

There is an old Chinese proverb that runs: "May you live in interesting times."

That is an understatement of what had transpired at Georgia Federal Bank during the past four years.

The bank had been converted from a mutual institution to a publicly held stock company in 1984.

At that time, J. B. Fuqua bought a personal interest in the company and joined the Board of Directors.

Georgia Federal then purchased First Family Financial Services from The First National Bank of Atlanta in 1985.

In April 1986 Fuqua Industries acquired all the stock of the company.

New management was then installed beginning in July of that year, and the company was restructured to functionally operate like a commercial bank.

It was put up for sale by Fuqua in late 1987 and remained in that status for almost 18 months.

First Financial Management then bought the company and closed on the deal in June 1989.

All of these events occurred while much of the thrift industry was rapidly sinking below the waves of turmoil from its financial instability, forcing a bevy of new regulations and regulators on the scene to salvage as much of the industry as possible.

Without question, the bank and all the different parties associated with it had experienced more than enough of the "interesting times," and were now inclined toward a period of stability.

It was definitely time to settle down and get on with life with our new owner. The bank's management and the frustrated bank employees were enthusiastic and excited about the acquisition and the future prospects for the company. We headed the bank in that direction, as quickly as feasible and got back to the task of running our business.

Our directorate was altered, after the acquisition was completed, with Fuqua and Klamon leaving the board along with John Zellars, who finally took his well-earned retirement.

Pat Thomas assumed the Chairman's role and I remained as the Chief Executive and became the Vice-Chairman. Bill Farr, upon joining the company, became President and Chief Operating Officer.

The remaining directors continued with the new owners and were highly supportive. We had an extremely qualified group of businessmen and professionals on our Board including, Sanford Orkin, a Personal Investor, William Suttles, Provost and Acting President of Georgia State University, James A Verbrugee, Chairman of the Finance Department, University of Georgia, Daniel Baker, CEO Crawford Long Hospital, Hugh Inman, President, Ruralist Press, and Douglas Schachner, Chief Financial Officer of FFMC.

Georgia Federal Bank, under new ownership, continued with its business plan. We worked diligently to merge our culture with FFMC and achieve the objectives established for the bank.

The strategy was to continue to grow the bank in its local markets and to emphasize the growth prospects of First Family Financial Services. The plan was logical and would ultimately reap nice dividends for our new owners.

Return on assets averaged about 80 to 90 basis points, or between $29 to $35 million in earnings annually, while FFMC owned the company. The bank's performance remained stable during this time, while much of the thrift industry continued to decline.

The operating mechanism to handle the credit card clearing and funds operation was implemented at the bank and served the purposes FFMC had predicted prior to the purchase of the company. The bank's data processing functions were integrated with the parent's operations, resulting in sizable cost reductions.

Considerable management efforts were made to realize the benefits from the identified pre-acquisition synergy opportunities existing among the companies in the FFMC organization. In addition, some new business opportunities for the bank were consummated with the customers of FFMC.

The cost reductions, income producing opportunities, and earnings from the Georgia Federal operation produced a nice return on investment for the corporation. However, the largest financial benefit would accrue to FFMC four years later, when the bank was sold to First Union Corporation in June 1993.

In the spring of each year the Corporate Challenge, a 3.5-mile run, was held in the streets in the central part of downtown Atlanta. Naturally, we encouraged our employees to participate and wear their bank designed T-shirt in the race.

The Manufactures Hanover Corporation, in New York City, had sponsored these popular races for a number of years. When they declined to continue with their sponsorship of the Atlanta event, we grabbed it.

Georgia Federal always had strong employee participation in the race. Naturally, this was accomplished by appropriately motivating and doing whatever it took to induce our employees to run in the race.

The bank had been awarded the first place participation prize several years in a row. We tried to make it a total company event and served refreshments and "partied" at the conclusion of each run to help induce interest and involvement.

After one of the race events, Maria Saporta, a business writer for the Atlanta Journal-Constitution newspaper, wrote an article about the race titled, "Motivated to run." In her column she accused me of strong-arming my employees into winning the participation award. She noted we had 853 staff members in Atlanta and 671 had run in the race, which had attracted over ten thousand runners that particular year.

She asked me how we were able to achieve such a high percentage of participants and I told her, which she quoted in her article, **"It was either through leadership or fear, but then I frequently get these issues confused."**

She has always enjoyed adding some controversy for the reader in her columns. Personally, I think she has done a fabulous job for the Atlanta readership since assuming her business-reporting role.

The first year the bank sponsored the race we were able to increase the number of participants, with lots of merchandising, by over 3,000 runners to a total of 13,000, which was a record for the event. However, the fun and games were about to end for Georgia Federal.

In mid-year of 1992 FFMC was contacted by First Union concerning their interest in purchasing the bank for their Georgia operations. At that time those holdings principally consisted of the First Railroad and Banking Company of Georgia organization, which had been acquired in 1986.

Many of the executives of our company were surprised when the discussions started. However, FFMC no longer needed the bank for its credit card operations. No restrictions had occurred as a result of the competitions' efforts to prohibit third-party processors from utilizing the funds clearing operation of the Federal Reserve System.

The timing was good for FFMC to consummate a sale and reap the benefits of a likely spike in the stock price.

The investment analysts would reason this disposition was a good decision, because the sale would eliminate unnecessary credit risk from the company's balance sheet.

FFMC could then fully concentrate on acquiring companies in the information services business, adding to their already large franchise. This strategy had strong appeal in the investment community.

First Union completed the due diligence and it appeared a deal was in the making. At the last minute it fell through, because of some minor issues involving the balance sheet of the bank and sales price.

Everyone went back to work thinking the crisis had passed, but another round of discussions were forthcoming in six months.

FFMC had made the decision to sell the bank for reasons noted, and sent a package of information on Georgia Federal to a number of prospective investors. Response initially was not great. Several months passed and no purchasers surfaced.

Then in late December, First Union came back to town with a horde of analysts to look once again at purchasing Georgia Federal. At 8 p.m. on December 22, 1992, while hosting a Christmas party for the bank senior executives at my home, I received a telephone call from Pat and was told the deal with First Union was back in play.

The message, from Thomas, was to assemble my staff immediately at the bank and commence the due diligence process. The party was over and we went back to work--- again

Within four days the deal was put together, a price agreed upon, and six months later, after the necessary regulatory approvals had been obtained, on June 15, 1993, First Union Corporation completed the acquisition of Georgia Federal.

Two significant events occurred permitting the deal to proceed without any outstanding issues.

First Financial had won approval to open a small credit card bank. This would ensure access to the Federal Reserve check clearing system in the event future restrictions was placed on third party processors. With this hurdle cleared, the company no longer needed to own a large financial institution, particularly; an S&L situated in a troubled industry.

Secondly, a deal was structured with First Associates, a large consumer finance operation based in Texas to purchase First Family Financial Services. First Union had no interest in buying our subsidiary. It did not fit into the long-range plans for their Georgia-based operations.

First Union had already acquired the second largest thrift in Georgia, Atlanta based Decatur Federal, in January 1993. With the inclusion of Georgia Federal, their bank operations in Georgia would now have $12 billion in assets and would be the second largest depository institution in the state. This had all been accomplished since the acquisition of First Railroad and Banking Company seven years earlier.

Georgia Federal Bank was purchased for approximately $279 million. The purchase price included cash of $154 million and a dividend from the bank to FFMC, at the close of the transaction, of $115 million.

First Family Financial Services was sold for approximately $225 million. The combined transaction was worth $500 million to FFMC.

Obviously, the acquisition of Georgia Federal had been a great investment for First Financial. The company had weathered the turmoil in the industry, their stock price had recovered from an initial decline when they bought the bank, and it had been sold at a propitious time.

FFMC had originally paid $235 million in 1989, when they bought Georgia Federal from Fuqua Industries, resulting in a healthy cash gain of about $265 million. The four-year earnings had also been positive, contributing over $100 million to the corporation's earnings during that period of ownership.

The cash from this transaction would fuel new growth opportunities for FFMC, during the following two years, and enable several significant acquisitions, including the purchase of The Western Union Corporation in 1994.

When the deal was finally inked, Pat Thomas and I made a commitment to Harold Hansen, the President of First Union Bank of Georgia, concerning the transition. Hansen was told this would be the easiest acquisition First Union had ever attempted.

My banking career was coming to an end and I wanted it finalized in a professional manner. Consequently, our staff at the bank, headed by Bill Farr and Don Stout, worked to ensure that no actions or decisions were made during the lengthy transition period that would unfavorably impact either company once the deal was completed.

When the process was finalized, Harold called Pat and told him how pleased he was with the cooperation of the bank and the ease of the conversion to First Union. Mission accomplished.

Endgame. This transaction basically concluded my 26-year banking career, 7 years at First National, 12 at First Georgia, and 7 at Georgia Federal. This smooth transition in selling the bank was my swan song in the final act.

Now, no longer a bank president, my new responsibilities would be as a Senior Executive Vice President and the Chief Operations Officer for FFMC. This would be a very different and challenging game to play. It was called Information Services.

Grantland Rice, in his sports poem, The Undefeated, wrote as follows: "When the one Great Scorer comes to mark against your name, he writes not whether you won or lost, but how you played the game.

Chapter Eleven
First Financial Management, Inc.

When First Financial purchased Georgia Federal in 1989 my role was expanded and I was made a member of the management team and a Senior Executive Vice President of the corporation. This would become a full time job after the bank was sold. At that time I was also assigned the responsibility as the chief operations officer.

The most interesting aspect of this role was my relationship with Pat Thomas, which had started in1968 when we were young, new employees at the First National Bank of Atlanta, fresh out of the military, and only recently employed at the bank. We immediately became friends as a result of our common backgrounds and interests.

Many noontime hours were spent running on the indoor, oval track at the downtown YMCA, and our careers had advanced somewhat on a parallel basis until 1986.

By then, FFMC had emerged as an entirely public company, was no longer under the control of First Railroad, and was beginning to become a real "climber" in the information services industry, ultimately becoming one of the largest in the nation.

Pat's achievements had placed him in a much senior and responsible role to me. The success and notoriety of FFMC was manifested by those efforts.

We had been friendly, but argumentative allies during our years at First Railroad. Our strong personalities and pride in the corporate accomplishments of the companies we managed fostered a willingness to speak our minds openly on any disagreements we had we each other or with senior management. Much to their chagrin, I must admit.

As a result of this "exuberant verbosity and theatrics," many people thought we were hostile enemies. In fact, we relished in the ability to create a more challenging, interesting, and creative management environment within First Railroad.

We saw this as a way to make the company better and certainly more stimulating, regardless of any fall-out or criticism we might personally experience from our contemporaries and senior executives. We would not hesitate to use dramatics to achieve these goals. Those tactics may not have been in our best interests personally, but they were effective.

Having been associates for many years was both a plus and a negative for me when FFMC bought Georgia Federal. If it had not been for our previous personal relationship and the integrity of that association, Thomas probably would not have been interested in purchasing the bank. That was the plus.

The negative was the same issues most people, under similar conditions, would have experienced. The ego adjustment of two contemporaries, whose roles had changed and placed one in a senior position over the other, followed by the conflict normally resulting from strong-willed personalities. There is nothing new in this analogy.

When FFMC announced the purchase of the bank, a creative writer for the Georgia Trend magazine penned an interesting article about our previous relationship and habits. The title was, **"Can Rambo and Red Man live Happily Together?"**

A summary of the article noted the following: "FFMC's purchase of Georgia Federal brings two of the biggest egos of Atlanta's financial industry together under one corporate roof. How long can Pat Thomas and Dick Jackson coexist in harmony?"

"Thomas collects Ferraris and speedboats and congenially offers guests a chew from his ever-present pouch of Red Man tobacco. Jackson is known as the 'Rambo' of banking and takes underlings on grueling wilderness survival weekends."

"The pair are old friends and share common interests, including a military background, a maniacal pursuit of physical fitness, and a habit of arriving at the office before dawn."

We had been highly competitive contemporaries dedicated to our individual operations, while operating at similar management levels in the same organization for 12 years.

This past relationship made it personally difficult to adjust from that association to a new boss-subordinate relationship.

It may have been just as trying for Pat. If it was, he didn't tell me or let it interfere with his plans in running the company. He had the proxies, power, and title.

All things considered, we managed through the situation until my retirement in 1995. Nevertheless, it was not an easy role to play, because I had been a CEO for 20 years and the master of my own counsel for much of that time.

Egos will always get in the way and create personal problems in most organizations. That is a known. However, if you make the decision to work for someone, do it with all the vigor, enthusiasm, and integrity that you can muster. If you determine you can't handle the situation and it stirs problems in your soul, requiring uncomfortable mental adjustments, get out as quickly as possible. You will be a better and more contented person, if the decision is made for the right reasons.

The history of FFMC started in 1971, when First Railroad & Banking Company formed a data processing subsidiary from their own internal operations to perform in-house computer work and to solicit processing from other financial institutions around the state.

Many commercial banks had entered into similar arrangements with client banks for the purpose of increasing fee-based revenues, and to leverage the excess capacity of their computer facilities.

FFMC, under Thomas's leadership, grew quickly over the next few years. In the early eighties, First Railroad with Pat's urging, elected to take First Financial public in 1983 by selling over half of the company's stock in the market.

At that time, FFMC had revenues of approximately $31 million and was providing computer-related services only to banks. In early 1984 the stock was valued at $14 per share.

From that time until 1989, when Georgia Federal was purchased, FFMC had sold the remainder of their stock in the public market and completed 27 acquisitions. Their revenue had grown to approximately $670 million with earnings of $57 million.

The basic business of bank processing continued to grow and the company expanded into several different lines of computer directed activity, including credit card processing, data preparation, data imaging, and mortgage loan accounting.

The acquisition of the bank provided FFMC with a direct link from their financial services operations to the Federal Reserve payments system, a large banking network, and a multi-state consumer finance operation.

From 1989 until 1993, when FFMC sold the Georgia Federal Operations, the corporation continued expanding its basic lines of business by increasing market penetration and making synergistic acquisitions.

In addition to the banking operations FFMC also owned the following companies:

NaBANCO, a credit card processing company based in Florida. TeleCheck, a check authorization and verification operation located in Houston. Nationwide Credit, a debt collection company, Microbilt, a computer terminal manufacturing operation, and First Image, a data imaging and microfilming operation. These three companies were based in Atlanta.

They also owned First Health Strategies in Richmond, Virginia, and First Health Services located in Salt Lake City. Both of these companies were in the health care business and involved in the establishment of care networks and health claims processing.

The Western Union Financial Services Company, based in New Jersey, was acquired in 1994 along with six smaller operations that were merged into the other major lines of business.

At the end of 1993, FFMC posted revenues of approximately $2 billion and pre-tax income of $216 million. Revenues and net income had both grown at a compound rate of over 30% since 1989, the year the bank was purchased.

The market capitalization of the company had risen from $1.0 billion in 1989 to $3.4 billion at the end of 1993, representing a compound growth rate of approximately 37%.

1994 would be the last full year of operations for FFMC, but it would be a very good one and indicative of the achievements the company had made since going public in 1983.

FFMC had become one of the largest Information Services Companies in the nation, while experiencing phenomenal success and growth in every financial measurement category.

Revenues had increased 9,100%, net income 8,800%, cash flow 7,000%, market capitalization 9,200% and shareholder equity 10,800%.

Recognition for these accomplishments were noted by several business publications in 1994 and was certainly well deserved, based on the progress the corporation had made during its 11-year existence. The accolades bestowed on the company included:

**Named as one of Fortune magazine's Most Admired.
Noted in Business Week as one of America's most
Valuable.
Named in Forbes magazine's 500 Most Valuable.
Noted in the Atlanta Journal-Constitution newspaper
as one of the Top Ten Best Businesses in Atlanta.**

The company reached its highest plateau in performance in every category in 1994. Revenues were $4 billion, and net income was $298 million. Shareholder equity was $1.4 billion and the market capitalization of the company at year-end was $4.2 billion.

Amazingly, FFMC had made over 100 acquisitions during the previous ten-year period and assimilated those successfully and profitably into the corporate operating structure. This feat, in conjunction with the other achievements, is probably without parallel in this business segment.

Divestitures, such as Georgia Federal, First Family, and the original business line of bank data processing were also accomplished without affecting the momentum of the company.

The purchase of The Western Union Company in 1994 added significantly to the stature, position, and name recognition of the corporation. With all the new additions to the various lines of business and focus on the original strategy of the company, FFMC was nicely postured to grow even more rapidly in the future.

One of the operating hallmarks of the company, and a principal reason FFMC performed so well, resulted from the financial discipline imposed by senior management.

Extensive financial analysis was performed monthly in all corporate subsidiaries by a group of in-house industry specialists. These were reviewed with the unit operating management to make certain each unit president had a good understanding of any performance problems or new profit opportunities existing within the individual business lines.

This process ensured all of the executives understood the dynamics of their business and why they were performing as they did. These monthly sessions could be grueling and time consuming, but they helped maintain focus on the key business issues.

The acquisition methodology was another process, which had been refined and closely adhered to when a new business opportunity or purchase was undertaken. These procedures had evolved over the years, as a result of the extensive activity in this area by the company.

Nothing was left to chance during due diligence, which was extremely well documented. The participating team members would present their findings to senior management during an extensive and detailed review session. At the conclusion of the analysis, the team would submit their personal recommendation "on a go or no go basis."

This group vote, although symbolic in nature, nevertheless fostered a commitment and a "bet your ass," or buy-in attitude on the final decision, which was based on the presented factual and analytical data gathered during the evaluation phase.

These processes were simply outstanding and the discipline to maintain them under all circumstances made it possible for FFMC to successfully undertake many diverse activities.

When 1995 started, I was unaware at the time, but within eight months I would be out of a job and undertaking early retirement.

My business responsibilities were rapidly becoming obsolete, meaning, "you're no longer needed." Actually, this sudden change would present me with great relief and contentment outside the daily grind of the corporate life, much to my surprise.

The transition was quite easy. Fortunately, I was able to maintain my personal self-esteem, a factor that seems to be a major obstacle for many executives when they are required to give up the "pomp and circumstance" of a high profile corporate position.

It seems apparent when a change is forthcoming in a company, either in ownership or management, there are signals transmitted that may appear transparent to many people. Those signs were beginning to occur at the FFMC headquarters during the first few months of 1995.

Senior executives can transmit intentions without realizing it by the tone or inflection of their voice at management meetings and by demonstrating a lessening of intensity in discussions, a shallow follow-up on decisions, and by unexplained absences from the office.

Today, the sale of a company is a way of life in corporate America. The best anyone can hope for, when their company is sold, is that they have gained enough knowledge, experience, and a good reputation as a professional to allow them go on to bigger and better things.

Of course, if the employee receives a significant monetary payoff from stock or an employment contract, a different set of issues evolve around their future and makes the entire situation more palatable.

Obviously, the most important consideration in any corporate transaction is the resultant affect it will have on the shareholders. Simply stated, is it a good deal for them or not?

By the end of the first quarter, discussions had started with a suitor, First Data Corporation, Inc., a company slightly larger than FFMC, but basically in similar lines of business.

These negotiations were not readily apparent to most people in the management structure, but signals were being transmitted, and some people believed it was in the best interests of all parties to put a deal together of some kind. In other words, we buy them or they buy us.--- They bought us.

I was not part of any discussions with the ultimate purchasers of FFMC. However, Pat Thomas and Tarlton Pittard, our talented chief financial officer, along with the others involved, did a superior job negotiating a proper deal for our shareholders, management, and for the continued employment of many of our unit executives and employees.

As a factual matter, I cannot recall any major employee reduction program being put into play after the company was purchased.

For the fifth time in my business career, June the month of brides and marriages would serve as a defining period in my destiny.

In **June 1995,** a corporate marriage was announced in a headline in the business section of the Atlanta Journal-Constitution newspaper. It read: "First Financial to Merge with Rival."

In **June 1993,** First Union completed the purchase of Georgia Federal from FFMC.

In **June 1989,** FFMC purchased Georgia Federal from Fuqua Industries.

On **June 13, 1986,** an article appeared announcing my acceptance of the CEO position at Georgia Federal Bank.

On **June 15, 1986,** the acquisition of First Railroad by First Union Corporation was announced.

First Data Corporation surprised all the analysts when they announced they would purchase FFMC with a $7.2 billion stock deal. There were many people who believed this was a grand transaction for both companies, but some analysts concluded the price was much too low, because of FFMC's past financial performance and market placement.

Under the proposed deal, the shareholders of FFMC would receive approximately $100 worth of First Data stock for each share of First Financial stock.

The day prior to the announcement our stock closed at $84 up $7.25, but was still obviously well below the final sales price.

Pat Thomas summed up the transaction appropriately, when he was quoted in a newspaper article: "This was strictly a business deal that was in the best interests of the shareholders---our shareholders got the premium (stock price) and their shareholders got the management."

First Financial did have excellent management talent in the company. Thomas, earlier in the year, had formed the Office of the Chairman, perhaps in anticipation of things to come. It consisted of himself as the Chairman, and included the following Vice Chairman, Tarlton Pittard, our highly capable chief financial officer, Steve Kane, the chief administrative officer, who was an excellent deal maker, Robert Anman, formerly the president of Western Union, who then held an operating management position in the company, and myself. Randy Hutto, a senior executive vice president and very knowledgeable attorney, was also a member of this group.

In addition, both our corporate staff and the line officers in the various units were extremely qualified and knowledgeable. Many of these people either stayed with First Data after the acquisition or accepted promising opportunities with other companies.

Since the deal was consummated, First Data Corporation has performed very well and has successfully integrated the various components of both companies into a unified, profitable, and growing organization in the Information Services industry.

The transaction closed in early October 1995. My retirement occurred at the end of August.

I chose to seek other adventures, mostly living part of the next seven years in the mountains around Sun Valley, Idaho and serving on various corporate boards of directors.

My insight had told me there would be no position available for me in the acquiring organization. Besides, this was my chance to do something different with my life at age 58.

After being acquired, by different companies, three times over the previous six years, the time was right and I was ready to move on to new opportunities and challenges.

There is a story about the former Prime Minister of Great Britain, Sir Winston Churchill, which best summed up my feelings at the time.

Churchill had the reputation of imbibing alcohol frequently during his life, and the tale originated at the time he was speaking to the British equivalent of the Women's Temperance Union.

One of the dear ladies in the audience commented that she was concerned about his drinking habits. She told the Prime Minister that she had roughly calculated, from various stories about him that he had consumed enough liquor during his life to fill the room they currently occupied halfway to the ceiling.

Sir Winston, never to be at a loss for words, looking first at the ceiling and then at the center of the wall, noticing the distance between the two points, sadly shaking his head, responded:

"So much to do and so little time in which to do it."

Chapter Twelve
ebank Financial Services, Inc.

The poet and writer, Alphonse Karr, has provided us with a quote that is profound in context and unique in perspective: **"The more things change, the more they remain the same."** The validity of this statement may be suspect to some people, but for me it has been unusually accurate.

In October 2000, at the request of the board of directors, my banking career was resurrected when I joined as Chairman of the Board, ebank.com, a two-year-old company owning a unitary S&L or Thrift, ebank, based in Atlanta.

The company had recently experienced severe financial problems, resulting from the consequences of mismanagement, troubled assets, and a fouled business strategy.

The status of the company was similar to the deteriorating situation at First Georgia Bank at the time I joined that organization 28 years earlier. Even the size of the two institutions were identical, approximately $100 million in assets. The major difference was the charter. The former was a commercial bank and the latter was a savings and loan or thrift organization.

The comparability of the problems and issues facing the two institutions were nearly identical, and echoed loudly the essence of Karr's quote.

My banking career had now come full circle. Starting with a problem company in 1974, I had once again become involved with an institution striving for survival, and that decision was also made of my own free will. **Lessons Learned the Hard Way:** The repeating character theme of my life.

After leaving the banking world in 1993, when Georgia Federal was sold, I had decided not to join any bank organizations. In the future, my focus and attention would be directed to companies not related to the financial services industry. I was seeking different exposures in order to broaden my base of knowledge in the corporate world.

However, a call to re-enter the banking world came clothed in an unsuspecting suit.

Jim Box had worked with me at First Georgia and Georgia Federal Banks, and had recently assumed the CEO position at ebank.com. The company name was changed on January 1, 2003 to ebank Financial Services, Inc. with only the bank retaining the name ebank.

He was replacing the former president, because the board had uncovered some financial problems and was frantically searching for a qualified candidate to provide new leadership and direction for the faltering company.

He inquired on behalf of the board by asking me to join the directorship and help with the recovery and stabilization of the institution.

After carefully examining the situation and meeting with the Office of Thrift Supervision, OTS, in Atlanta, I agreed to his request and joined the company, as the Chairman, in the fall of 2000.

The Holding Company and Thrift had been in operation for approximately two years. The company was organized as a public corporation in 1998. At that time, this was the largest initial public stock offering (IPO) in Georgia for a start-up financial institution. The company had raised approximately $13.7 million in that subscription.

The initial strategies established for the company were as follows:

(1) Implement an Internet presence with a banking web site.
(2) Develop an Internet-enabled ATM network.
(3) Establish Internet affiliations with community banks across the nation.
(4) Locate 24 banking centers in key growth cities nationwide with small-to-medium disenfranchised corporate banking customers, who have high Internet usage and strong business growth.
(5) Primarily operate from a single "bricks and mortar" location in Vinings, a suburb of Northwest Atlanta.

The strategic business plan looked intriguing on paper, and some stockbrokers and investors thought this was an idea whose time had come.

However, the reality of reaching across the country and establishing a meaningful banking network of loan production offices in distant markets from Atlanta, albeit, tied together through the Internet, would require significant capital investment, which the bank did not have immediately available, even with the success in the initial public offering.

The plan would necessitate heavy expenditures for technology development, the hiring of qualified banking personnel, and ultimately be supported by sound financial and management controls to monitor expenses and progress.

Unfortunately, the bank initiated the development, hired the people, and attempted to raise more capital in the markets, but forgot to implement the control system. Therein was the problem.

The glamour of the dot.com world and unique strategy did attract investors and the stock gained in favor reaching a per share price of approximately $17 six months after the bank opened the doors. The stock sold for $10 per share in the initial offering.

Sizable investments were also made to build a web site, acquire the necessary computer resources, and open a main office in the upscale and bucolic Vinings area of Atlanta.

These capitalized expenditures would require several years of write-offs, or non-cash expenses, to amortize the investment on the books of the company. This would unfavorably impact the earnings capability during the critical time the company was attempting to grow and obtain profitability.

After depleting over half of the capital through marketing, capital acquisition costs, and general operating losses the company attempted to raise additional equity in early 2000. Unfortunately, the markets softened and ebank.com was unable to structure a financial deal without substantially diluting the original stockholder's investment or adding significant interest expenses.

There was one final shoe to fall in the company's deteriorating saga. It was the realization that the prospective customers in the financial markets were not ready to convert their transactions and change their banking orientation to an electronic financial network.

This same attitude seemed to prevail for other financial institutions with a similar strategy.

Some of the Internet banks, which had started life with exciting prospects, rapid deposit growth, and inflated stock prices, began to settle back into this reality. This occurred, because the market readjusted its thinking and valuation about these unique banking operations.

The dwindling stock values, in conjunction with the questionable on-line strategy, began to suddenly beg the question regarding the viability for these new revolutionary Internet products.

Also, the evolving dot.com environment seemed to clearly demonstrate that although the prospects for Internet banking activities held great promise, they had not arrived as many pundits had previously forecasted.

Prospective investors were not willing to pay-up or gamble their money in "hope springs eternal" for this business model.

The Internet banking strategy was flawed, or so it seemed, and would not accomplish the objectives originally established by ebank.com or other similar institutions around the country.

The expenditures for the implementation of the business plan, coupled with the inappropriate expense controls, and management's inexperience placed the bank in a serious financial condition with an impaired capital position as 2000 came to a close.

An immediate change of management was mandated by the board and encouraged by the regulatory authority, the OTS, when the problems were finally uncovered.

The new CEO, Jim Box, was brought on board to restore the company to respectability and profitability. Subsequently, several new directors, with financial or banking backgrounds were added to the board to assist with industry guidance and improve the image of the company in the market.

With the emphasis placed on controls in today's highly violate corporate market, all companies must ensure they have the management experience and the attention and guidance of a qualified and dedicated directorate at all times.

The first steps taken by the new management team was to implement a viable control system in the company.

This action was followed by the introduction of an aggressive expense reduction program.

The loan portfolio was closely evaluated and received continuously monitoring by key management lending officers to minimize prospective losses.

A completely new staff, with banking experience, was ultimately hired over the next few months.

In addition, a program to raise capital was initiated and over $5.5 million of preferred stock was successfully added to the equity accounts of the company in the early months of 2001.

This creative private placement preferred stock offering was managed and sold by the Atlanta based investment firm, Attkisson, Carter, & Akers.

The preferred stock adequately filled the hole in the capital accounts of the company, which had been created by the indiscriminate investments in capital projects and excessive expenses.

Now, adequately capitalized and with good management, qualified bank employees, and controls in place ebank.com could institute a different strategy by growing the bank in a more traditional and conservative manner.

The board and management determined the focus should be on building the business from a single location in Vinings, and utilizing the sophisticated Internet capability for limited deposit gathering and the sale of a few select products.

All expansion considerations would be delayed, until the bank was operating profitably and had accumulated the capital and sustained income to support future growth opportunities.

This was a major deviation from the original strategy. The new objectives centered on building the business along more conventional lines. This has been a proven approach for many start-up financial institutions over the years.

Additionally, it was decided to play to our strength and concentrate on providing excellent service and senior management attention to our customer base. Management believed the bank's staff could concentrate on these sales features and materially affect a positive reaction in the market.

The larger institutions, because of their bureaucracy and size are unable to play this part of the game effectively.

Also, the bank would seek-out only those future business opportunities that could be leveraged with the current operations and were consistent with our thrift charter. There would be no outside the box, or crazy schemes, whatsoever, drafted into our operation by any source.

When 2002 started, management had planned for the bank to be profitable for the year. Mr. Greenspan, the Chairman and other members of the Federal Reserve Board, prompted by the subdued economy, promoted different mandates, specifically lowering the Federal funds lending rate 11 times over the following 12 month period.

Although necessary to the economic well being of our nation, these rate reductions dashed the company's hopes for profitability, as the earning assets, specifically loans, re-priced much faster than the liabilities or deposits. This resulted in a timing and rate imbalance between the yield on loans and cost of funds.

In essence, the earnings on loans dropped much more rapidity than the cost of the liabilities, which funded those assets.

The unplanned difference in spread between these two major balance sheet items cost us our profitability for the year, and only now, because of a better equalization in the rate structure, are we beginning to make the financial progress we had planned previously.

Nevertheless, the company was able to reestablish its position in the marketplace, implement a solid expense control system, effectively market its products, and manage the loan portfolio satisfactory through the economic downturn.

In addition, ebank.com made an acquisition of a highly profitable boutique investment firm; Atlanta based Peachtree Capital Corporation.

This was an integrated financial services company offering investment advice, financial planning, and securities/insurance brokerage services.

Bank management was hopeful they could leverage the customer bases of both companies in the cross-sell of products between ebank and Peachtree Capital. This tactic could contribute significantly to the growth and profitability of both operations.

Unfortunately, we were unable to capitalize on the strategy and fully achieve our expectations with this plan. As a result, the decision was made to sell the company back to the original owners at the close of 2002. However, Peachtree Capital did contribute profitably to the overall financial position during the company's ownership.

This was a difficult decision. The plan was not working as designed, and the board of directors elected to take action rather than pursue a strategy that was apparently destined for eventual failure.

Our executives and staff have performed admirably during these past two stressful years and have resolved some difficult and time-consuming issues, while continuing to improve the overall effectiveness of the company.

Many of the original Board of Directors have "stayed the course," and along with the new additions to the directorate are providing renewed enthusiasm, fresh perspective, and intense energy in the pursuit of the company's current goals.

The future does offer solid prospects for ebank, but we will need to "stick to our knitting," and stay focused on those things we know and do well to ensure a sustainable success with our operations.

We are now sufficiently experienced, bloodied by the past, and savvy enough to follow-through with our current plans, and deliberately, but carefully, climb the mountain.

With the start of 2003, the company's name was changed to ebank Financial Services, Inc. to more clearly identify us in the marketplace and reflect the nature of our business.

The company is now profitable and should experience a satisfactory year financially, if current conditions prevail and no uncontrollable or unexpected situations occur.

Additionally, the management team is now in the process of initiating some progressive financial engineering tactics with the balance sheet, which will be of great assistance to the future performance of the company.

This recent involvement in the dot.com world has provided a staggering and overwhelming education in a short period of time. It is a difficult business to comprehend and manage, because it is new, can be complicated, and the business model is somewhat undefined. It will most likely remain under some amount of scrutiny and development for the next few years.

Peanuts, the cartoon character, probably offered a humorous and interesting insight for many companies in today's world with one of his famous philosophical meanderings when he said: **"We are now surrounded by insurmountable opportunities."**

However, my description for ebank's future would be similar to an Army General's response at the time his unit was surrounded by the Germans in the Battle of the Bulge.

During the heavy fighting, when the combat situation was deteriorating, he was asked about his current status and responded as follows: **"They have crushed our front, enveloped our flanks, and penetrated our rear. We will attack."**

Observations

Yogi Berra, the famous manager of both the New York Yankees and Mets and a member of the Baseball Hall of Fame, has developed a kind of "guru" reputation over the years. This occurred because of his irrelevant and profound comments on various subjects, many about the game of baseball.

Unlike many other pundits, his statements are typically full of mixed metaphors, confusing analogies, and hidden meanings.

Notwithstanding, the careful listener not only finds humor and insight wrapped within his sayings, but with careful examination finds his comments really quite rational.

His most widely known and famous quote occurred when the Yankees were losing a game in the late innings, and he responded to a question about their chance of winning by saying: **"It ain't over till it's over."** The comment is indicative of the nature of his typical ramblings and prognostications.

Another example of his wisdom was demonstrated when Yogi accepted his first manager's position of a major league baseball team.

As he had no previous experience in that role, the sports writers questioned him at great length about his qualifications. Particularly, they wanted to know how he was going to develop his then non-existent managerial expertise.

Berra responded to the inquiring writers with one of his "Yogiisms" by telling them: **"You can observe a lot by just watching."**

Yogi's comment, perhaps confusing to some people, is appropriately indicative of the educational method that I have primarily employed during my years as a student, athlete, military officer, and business executive.

This identical learning technique worked for me in my pursuit of knowledge. I have diligently observed and read everything possible about successful people in the exploit of their individualism, talents, beliefs, and values.

Their personal characteristics have inspired me throughout my life and I have attempted to emulate them at every opportunity.

Continually assembling these so-called "pearls of wisdom" over the years, and blending them with my own experiences, both successful and not-so-successful, I have developed a compendium of principles and practices that have served as useful guidelines during the different aspects of my life.

The following statements are a compilation of my notes and contain in some diluted and altered format the thoughts, sayings, and advice of many successful and prominent people.

Working within this context, I have attempted to dramatize them as much as possible for affect, recall, and practical use.

The application of these points will not necessarily ensure success for any person or organization. However, it is my "somewhat bias opinion" that if utilized and practiced properly they can help create positive and lasting results in most situations.

Always take the high ground---and hold it. It is the best defensive position and provides the greatest observation. Do not aim for anything less in life. When you gain your objective or reach the pinnacle of your success, don't stop doing the things that got you there, because the enemy or the competition might just overrun your position.

Don't make "no sudden moves," especially when you're in a minefield. Know your terrain and markets, your enemies' or competitors' capabilities and strengths. Anticipate changes in both yours and the aggressor's plans and direction. Think about your next move; even your next step.

Commitments matter. Always do what you say you're gonna do when you say you're gonna do it. People are counting on you to carry out your mission. If you fail to execute, the entire plan or relationship may be jeopardized.

Don't be afraid to be afraid. These attitude keeps you on your toes and it makes you want to learn more and stay current. But, don't ever show fear or indecision to your troops. Keep your personal demeanor under control at all times.

Stay lean and mean, physically and mentally. This gives you the edge when things really get tough. Your enemy or competition may not be able to maintain the same level of energy and momentum. It helps keep you alert and ready for most any contingency.

Be too stupid to know when to quit. Success many times is nothing more than hanging on when everyone else has let go. Let the other guy quit. If you do, you will be replaced. If you quit the other people in your organization will follow the example. Sometimes it's possible to talk ourselves out of winning. Listen to your better instincts and go for the jugular every time.

If you won't do it, why should anyone else? Don't be afraid to get your hands dirty. Pitch in and help whenever you can. Your troops will respect you more and follow you to hell and back.

When the enemy is in range so are you. Never take anything for granted. If you can get to your enemy or the competition, they can get to you. Think about it.

Use the 7 P's of planning. Proper Prior Planning Prevents Piss-Poor Performance. Always do you homework, anticipate, communicate, and then execute. No plan is ever complete; it will need constant updating with the changing conditions.

The higher the monkey climbs the more his ass is exposed. As the leader you will always be scrutinized for your actions. That is the price paid for success. You must be able to tolerate the pain, carry out your mission, and win the objective.

Do as I say and do. Always set the example. Your people are watching everything you do and taking the measure of your actions. If you demand, plan, and practice excellence in your organization it will become a way of life.

The diversion you are ignoring may be the main attack, or if the attack is going really well, you may be in an ambush. Keep on top of issues in your organization. Stay abreast of the situation and never, never take anything for granted. Don't get too comfortable with your situation, because that's when you lose your ass. Always try to know what the enemy or competition is doing, and anticipate the next move. Yours and theirs.

A Fubar is a way of life. (Fucked-up beyond absolute recognition) Unexpected miscues will always plague your plans. Screw-ups happen with the best of people and under the best of circumstances. Don't be surprised or disappointed. Always have a contingency plan.

Nobody is perfect, including you. Keep your sense of humor and for God's sake don't get the big head. Nobody is indispensable. But, if you think you are, remember the old adage: "Put your finger into a bowl of water, and then remove it, and notice the hole that it left."

1000% improvement is possible. Ridiculous, no one can improve that much. But, you can improve on and in everything you do by some percentage. 1% improvement in 1000 different things is 1000%. Keep an open mind on ways to live your life.

Don't schedule visits to "SOMEDAY ISLE." It is a terrible place to spend time. Procrastination will never solve any problems or help achieve personal objectives. It's too damned easy to waste your time by putting off those things that are important or difficult by telling yourself **Someday I'll** get that work done. Or **Someday I'll** enroll in that class, or **Someday I'll** start that personal project, or whatever it is that should be started, particularly, if you know in your mind it should be done now.

Get outside the box. Keep your perspective open and fresh. Reinvent yourself over and over so that you can keep growing. Don't just think outside the box, **"live outside the box."** Life will be more interesting, stimulating, and exciting.

KISS---Keep it simple stupid. Declutter your life and right size at every opportunity; get rid of the crap. Keep your mental and physical closets "squared away" all the time. Focus on those things that are important in your life, and don't even think about making simple things difficult. Let the bureaucrats do that.

Don't let anyone steal your dreams or curb your passions. Carl Sanders had a sign in his office, an old Roman phrase that read, **"Illegitimis Non Carborundum."** Translated, it reads, **"Don't let the bastards wear you down."** It makes the point. Stick with your plan, don't worry about what other people say, and think. And don't let anyone drag you down to his or her level.

Don't let yourself suffer root rot. Most things are not as bad as you may initially think. You can probably recall worse times in your life. Today's problem may seem inconsequential in comparison. It's important to remember where you came from and how you got to the place where you are now. Keep doing those things that helped you grow. Stop doing the things that didn't.

Be a strategic explorer, and don't be afraid of going on expeditions into unknown territory. This is the way to learn new ideas and different approaches in problem solving and life in general. Venture forward at every opportunity, open your mind, don't be a stick in the mud or allow the creeping "we have always done it that way" syndrome to affect your positive thinking and adventuresome spirit.

Winners win because they believe they can. They are also better trained, more disciplined, motivated, and hungrier than their rivals. When the moment of decision or action arises, they have trained themselves mentally to be ready and prepared to take advantage of the situation and "win the day." Winners always believe they will eventually overcome any obstacle. It's a mindset and a self-fulfilling prophecy.

What you think determines your behavior more than what you know. Believe in yourself. Your confidence and positive feelings about yourself are as important as those things learned in a textbook. What and how you think will determine your performance. If you believe you can do something, you probably can. If you don't think you can, you won't. Either way you will be right. Ask yourself, "What do I think about most of the time?" Your answer may be revealing.

Don't forget the bad news and good news. The good news is that you can start any new initiative within minutes after you make up your mind to do it. The bad news is you never finish improving your life, job, marriage, or anything else that is important and worthwhile.

Use it and you lose it. Don't be cheap, but be tight-fisted with your funds. Establish a mind-set of expense control and good personal budgeting techniques. All funds spent should provide a return on investment of some kind. Do not let your precious dollars be used for erratic or irrational schemes.

Money should be invested in the business and not in oil paintings hanging on the wall. As a banker I was always observant of the physical plant of a company during my visits. The company's money, and especially the bank's funds, should primarily be invested in the business, and not in fancy and expensive "toys" for the executive's pleasure or exotic office fixtures that are more for show than profit.

No Company ever went broke making a profit. Your prime mandate and responsibility to your shareholders is to make money on their investment. Anything less is not acceptable. Don't create budgets; formulate profit plans for your company.

There they go, I must hasten to catch them for I am their leader. Stay in the foreground and not in the background. You can't lead effectively from the rear. Your people want to know that you're committed. The actions that you take will inspire them to reach greater heights in their work.

Cheerleaders have all the fun. A manager's job, among many responsibilities, is to motivate their people to reach the desired objectives. Recognize, reward, and acknowledge accomplishments on a regular basis. Praise for a job well done should be a common practice. Look for people doing things right. Constant criticism and lack of attention will dull employee performance and create resentment that may be impossible to overcome. Praise, praise, praise, and don't forget to say; **"Thank you."**

Only toads should live under mushrooms. Don't keep your people in the dark. Tell them what's going on at every opportunity.

Communicate frequently and make certain they understand the mission and the objectives of the organization. Don't you like to know what's going on? So do your people. Keep them informed.

Make work fun. We spend most of our waking hours on the job. Make it enjoyable. It should be as much fun and interesting as any other activity. Find ways to enhance performance by creating an environment that promotes job satisfaction. Don't act as if you were weaned on a pickle. Create and implement activities within the work arena for your employees that will keep them smiling, amused and happy. Don't worry, your people will still get the job done, probably much better than they would if they worked for some hard ass. Ask yourself this question. Do I have to leave the job to find enjoyment? If you do, so do your people.

Build fires to put them out. When you need a crisis to get people's attention, start one. When things become slow and lethargy starts to ease into your organization that's the time to step up the activity and get the adrenaline pumping. Start some new initiatives that will involve the entire staff, or shorten time frames on projects to speed-up employee participation. The main thrust should be to keep minds and hands occupied at all times to ensure that your organization is conditioned and ready for action.

Practice being a monomaniac with a mission. Your total dedication and commitment to the task is critical, if it is to be accomplished properly. A half-assed approach will not achieve the desired result. Get the job done and do whatever it takes. Be proud of your success. Your employees will feel the same pride in their efforts and they will emulate your enthusiasm.

Run like Hell all the time. Your speed and positive mental attitude determines how fast your employees will run. Don't procrastinate on important things. If you make the wrong decision, make another decision. It is impossible to be correct all the time. Management is employed to evaluate, decide, implement, and take risks. Do you do those things routinely?

Fulfill the prophecy. Don't accept defeatism. Believe in yourself and shape your destiny to achieve those things that are important to you. You are as good as you think you are.

You become what you think about. What are the thoughts that course through your head most of the time? They will direct your personal future. Keep your thinking focused and on the target.

Finally, keep moving forward. When you stop, you're finished. Aim for the stars. You may not reach them, but you might get to the mountaintop. And that's the place you need to be.

Printed in the United States
65334LVS00008BA/11

9 781418 429263